The
BOYDS COLLECTION LTD.

The Bearstone Collection®
The Folkstone Collection®
The Dollstone Collection™
The Shoe Box Bears™
and
Boyds Plush Animals

Secondary Market Price Guide
and Collector Handbook

SECOND EDITION

Wilson With Love Sonnets
Market Value (1E) – $520

Grenville The Santabear
Market Value (1E) – $520

The most valuable retired pieces in The Bearstone Collection:
Wilson With Love Sonnets (#2007) and Grenville The Santabear (#2030)

Collectors' Publishing would like to thank Harry Croft, publisher of "Bear Tales & Trails" newsletter (Palatine, IL), Boyds Bears experts Janet & Ed Hymes (Jacksonville, IL), Mary Jo Truax (Ridgeview, SD) and all the Boyds collectors and retailers who contributed their valuable time to assist us with this book. Also many thanks to the great people at The Boyds Collection Ltd.

This publication is *not* affiliated with The Boyds Collection Ltd.® or any of its affiliates, subsidiaries, distributors or representatives. Any opinions expressed are solely those of the authors, and do not necessarily reflect those of The Boyds Collection Ltd. "The Bearstone Collection®" and "The Folkstone Collection®" are registered trademarks of The Boyds Collection Ltd. "The Dollstone Collection™," "Yesterday's Child™" and "The Shoe Box Bears™" are trademarks of The Boyds Collection Ltd. Product names and product designs are the property of The Boyds Collection Ltd., Gettysburg, PA. Artwork used with permission.

Front cover (left to right): "Thayer," *Boyds plush;* "Bailey . . . Poor Ol' Bear," *The Boyds Collection;* "Michelle With Daisy . . . Reading Is Fun," *The Dollstone Collection.*
Back cover (top to bottom): "Egon . . . The Skier," *The Folkstone Collection;* "Wilson With Love Sonnets," *The Bearstone Collection;* "Edmund," *Boyds plush;* "Candice With Matthew . . . Gathering Apples," *The Dollstone Collection;* "Gertrude 'Gertie' Grizberg," *The Shoe Box Bears.*

Managing Editor:	Jeff Mahony	Art Director:	Joe T. Nguyen
Associate Editor:	Mike Micciulla	Staff Artist:	Scott Sierakowski
Editorial Assistants:	Gia C. Manalio		
	Katie M. Adams		

ISBN 1-888914-05-X

Collectors' Publishing Co., Inc.
598 Pomeroy Avenue
Meriden, CT 06450
http://www.collectorspub.com

CONTENTS

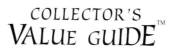
COLLECTOR'S
VALUE GUIDE™

CONTENTS

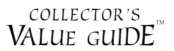
COLLECTOR'S
VALUE GUIDE™

Introducing The Collector's Value Guide™

Welcome to the second edition of The Boyds Collection Ltd. Collector's Value Guide! Though they make their home deep in the heart of Gettysburg, Pennsylvania, the Boyds Bears can be found in collectible and gift shops all over the country. The Boyds Collection Ltd. is bursting with unique and exciting ideas in their line of stuffed plush animals as well as in the resin Bearstones, Folkstones, Dollstone and Shoe Box Bears collections. As the line continues to grow, collectors are finding that there are quite a few questions that arise in the world of Boyds collectibles, such as:

- What are the new pieces this year?

- If a piece is no longer available in stores, how can I get it?

- What do the numbers on the bottom of my pieces mean?

- Is it a good idea to purchase insurance for my collection?

- What is my own collection really worth?

The answers to these questions, as well as many more, are just pages away. Inside the value guide, you will find full-color photos of Boyds resin figurines and plush animals, as well as essential information such as the issue year, item number and whether the piece is retired or currently available. Collectors in search of those hard-to-find pieces will be walked through the secondary market and those concerned with protecting their collection will learn the basics of insuring collectibles.

Collectors who are interested in the value of their pieces will love the value guide section, which lists secondary market values for retired pieces as well as early editions of current pieces. The value guide is designed as a worksheet on which you can record the market prices of your individual pieces in order to find out the total value of your collection. These prices have been gathered from a wide range of sources from all over the country, and are a benchmark that collectors can use to price their pieces for resale, for insurance purposes or just for fun. The easy-to-use Collector's Value Guide makes collecting Boyds Bears more fun than ever!

COLLECTOR'S
VALUE GUIDE™

Boyds Figurines Overview

Yer Ol' Uncle Bean

The Boyds Collection Ltd. was established not by a founding father, but by an uncle – "Yer Ol' Uncle Bean," that is! With several years of design and retail experience behind him, Gary Lowenthal first delved into the teddy bear world in 1987 by introducing a line of lovable plush animals. After designing and naming several hundred critters, Lowenthal was ready to bring his furry friends to new heights, and in 1993, a collection of resin figurines based on those loveable plush characters hit the stores – and The Bearstone Collection was born!

While the success of The Boyds Collection Ltd. has grown even beyond Lowenthal's expectations, the company retains its small, family-run feel. One big reason for this is Lowenthal's unique wit and offbeat charm, evident in the various aliases he uses ("G.M.," "Yer Ol' Uncle Bean," "The Head Bean Hisself"). His familiar, "goofing around" style makes collectors feel like they're part of an ever-growing Boyds family. And family is a very big part of The Boyds Collection Ltd. – if you know Boyds, you know the Lowenthals! Prominent plush and resin characters are named after Lowenthal's family: his wife Justina, daughter Bailey and son Matthew (he even named a character for his daughter's best friend, Emily). With four creative resin collections to choose from, collectors can join the Boyds family any way they wish!

The Boyds Bears Family Tree

The Bearstone Collection®

Folkstone Collection®

THE DOLLSTONE COLLECTION™

THE SHOE BOX BEARS™

The Bearstone Collection®

The very first "branch" of the Boyds family tree, The Bearstone Collection, debuted in 1993. Collectors familiar with the plush bears will recognize some familiar characters in this collection of resin figurines. The Bearstones depict the antics of bears, rabbits, moose and all sorts of other critters, who spend their time baking pies, taking romantic strolls, playing checkers and generally having fun. Since 1993, the collection has grown to 107 figurines (75 current, 32 retired). With 13 new figurines for early 1997 and more to come later in the year, the Bearstones have become one of the fastest-growing collectibles ever.

One reason for the incredible popularity of the Bearstones is the warm, comfortable look of the figurines; the rough textures and earthy color tones capture the very same familiarity that Gary Lowenthal spreads through his appearances at collectible shows and on the television shopping network, QVC. Many collectors are also attracted to the family themes that are reflected in heartwarming figurines depicting tea parties, newlyweds strolling arm-in-arm and expectant mothers pondering names for the "future arrival."

Although Lowenthal never intended his bear figurines to become a collectible item, thousands of collectors have said differently! An important part of the "collectibility" of the Bearstones is the edition numbers on the bottoms of the figurines ("1E," "2E," etc.). While there currently are 3,600 pieces in every Bearstone edition (except for *Holiday Pageant Series* pieces, which have 7,200 to every edition), The Boyds Collection Ltd. has indicated that the number will change in the near future. (For a detailed discussion of edition numbers, see *Secondary Market Overview*.)

The Bearstone Collection also includes 10 ornaments (seven current); seven waterglobes (five current); five votive candle holders; and the ever-fashionable Bearwear pins. Recently, The Boyds Collection Ltd. has spread its unique warmth and wit to our cousins up north, as several figurines have been made exclusively for stores in Canada. Beloved Bearstone characters can also be found in a series of waterglobes and music boxes produced by the San Francisco Music Box Company.

COLLECTOR'S
VALUE GUIDE™

Boyds Figurines Overview

The Folkstone Collection®

The second branch and "strange cousins" of the Boyds family tree, The Folkstone Collection is Lowenthal's attempt at traditional folk art – with a quirky Boyds twist! Like the Bearstones, these whimsical figurines feature a hodge-podge of fun-loving animals, along with angels, snowmen and Santas. Most of the Folkstones are "pencil-style" figurines (about 7 1/2" tall), except for the Santa figurines, which are (appropriately) wider. (FYI: It is assumed that none of the Folkstones are based on members of the Lowenthal family – we hope!)

The big news for The Folkstone Collection is the arrival of the Wee Folkstones, a series of gnomes, elves, faeries and guardian angels, complete with wings and their own special tasks ("'Electra' Angelbyte . . . Angel Of Computer Training"). These new releases reflect a trend toward smaller, "normal" sized figurines, including the very first shelf-sitters in the collection. Four of these new pieces debuted on QVC in January, with special markings on the bottom. Including the new Wee Folkstones, there are a total of 75 figurines (65 current), 10 ornaments, two waterglobes and several pins. Like the Bearstones, the Folkstones have 3,600 pieces to each edition, while the Wee Folkstones have 9,600 per edition.

The Dollstone Collection™

One of the more popular of Boyds' recent offerings, The Dollstone Collection brings a touch of elegance and finery to The Boyds Collection Ltd. These endearing figurines have a smoother finish than the Bearstones and Folkstones and are an instant tug on the heartstrings, as they depict wide-eyed girls from different historical periods holding their favorite dolls and teddy bears. In addition to the high level of detail and loving expressions, the Dollstones have captured the hearts of collectors with their return to days of innocence, when their best doll friends shared in their adventures. There have been 25 Dollstone figurines, with all but one currently available, and there are 4,800 pieces for every edition.

Boyds Figurines Overview

While the Dollstones officially appeared in stores in 1996, the first four figurines actually debuted on QVC in the fall of 1995. Many Dollstones have been introduced on the shopping channel since then, and these all feature special "Premier Edition" markings on the bottoms. Among the notable "firsts" for this charming collection is the first figurine featuring an African-American girl ("Natalie With Joy . . . Sunday School"), as well as the first Dollstone piece to feature Lowenthal's daughter Bailey. As a special honor, "The Amazing Bailey . . . 'Magic Show At 4'" is the Dollstone limited edition figurine for 1997 and is based on a charming event in Bailey Lowenthal's "playtime past."

The Shoe Box Bears™

It's only appropriate that the latest addition to the Boyds family is an entire family in its own right! Meet the Grizbergs, a group of stylish relations of the Bearstones, who go by the collective name of The Shoe Box Bears. These six playful, poseable bears are fully jointed and known as the "movers and shakers" of The Boyds Collection Ltd. (that is, they can really move!). From the family patriarch, "Augustus 'Griz' Grizberg" down to the flighty young daughter "Maisey 'The Goil' Grizberg," The Shoe Box Bears are some of the more personable and creatively-named bears around. Like their Bearstone cousins, these bears are marked with edition numbers; there are 6,000 pieces to every Shoe Box Bears edition.

These jointed figurines require a bit more care than their Bearstone cousins: the arms and legs are connected with rubber bands and collectors should be careful not to turn them around in circles or they could break. (Also, it's important to gently tug the arms and legs outward before moving them so as not to scratch the joint areas.) While they may have this "high maintenance" reputation amongst their peers, The Shoe Box Bears are a delightful addition to the growing Boyds family tree.

What's New

The Bearstone Collection®

This section highlights the new Bearstone figurine releases for 1997. It's a monumental year for the The Boyds Collection Ltd. as it leaps into the future with the milestone events of Bailey and Edmund's graduation, and introduces Boyds' first shelf sitter.

FIGURINES

Ariel & Clarence . . . As The Pair O' Angels (set/2) . . . These two little angels have strapped on their halos (even though Ariel's is just a bit off center, although it makes a heavenly earring) and are ready to grace the stage of the Holiday Pageant with their celestial message, "Believe."

Ariel & Clarence . . . As The Pair O' Angels (set/2) – #2411
Holiday Pageant Series

Bailey . . . The Graduate – Carpe Diem **and** *Edmund . . . The Graduate – Carpe Diem* . . . It's a glorious day for the Bearstone family as they celebrate Bailey and Edmund's graduation! All that lugging textbooks around and all night study sessions have paid off and both hold their diplomas proudly (and tightly with both hands – they've worked hard for this!). With their faithful teddy bears near-by and packed suitcases almost bursting at the seams, these two graduates are ready for all the adventures that the future holds for them.

Bailey . . . The Graduate – Carpe Diem – #227701-10

Edmund . . . The Graduate – Carpe Diem – #227701-07

Bailey . . . Poor Ol' Bear . . . Bailey is feeling a bit under the weather – not only is her arm in a sling, but she has a really bad cold too! Fortunately, she is her own little nurse with her medical book, bottles of bear aspirin, honey and a cold compress. It looks like this little bear will feel better in no time.

Bailey . . . Poor Ol' Bear – #227704

COLLECTOR'S
VALUE GUIDE™

Bruce . . . As The Shepherd . . . This tattered shepherd may not have riches to offer the holy couple but what he will give them is a gift unlike any other: a safe haven for the birth of a king. With lamb in hand, this furry thespian is ready to make his humble offerings in the Holiday Pageant.

Bruce . . . As The
Shepherd – #2410
Holiday Pageant Series

Buzz . . . The Flash . . . He's got the ball, he's dribbling down the court, he's just about to reach the foul line and . . . ooops. This hare may have perfected his jump shot but he hasn't quite mastered the task of tying his shoes!

Buzz . . . The Flash
– #227706

Essex . . . As The Donkey . . . Essex has finally landed a very important (and heavy) role in the Holiday Pageant! A donkey's walk isn't as easy as it looks and Essex is getting a little help coordinating his steps with a string tied from his left foot to his right paw. Never fear though, he's a quick learner and it won't be long before he's ready to carry Mary and Joseph safely into Jerusalem (silently he hopes that this action is a mere stage direction – such a little donkey can only carry so much weight!).

Essex . . . As The
Donkey – #2408
Holiday Pageant Series

The Flying Lesson . . . This End Up (LE-1997) . . . A brave little bear has just earned his wings through the "'Heavenly Home' Flight Training Kit." This would-be angel flies around in circles high above the heads of his teachers and admirers to the tune of "When You Wish Upon a Star." Limited to one year of production, "The Flying Lesson . . . This End Up" is the first musical figurine in The Boyds Collection Ltd.

The Flying Lesson . . .
This End Up (LE-1997)
– #227801

What's New

Humboldt . . . The Simple Bear . . . Humboldt, who was first introduced into the Boyds family as a plush bear, makes his debut in 1997 as a resin figurine. Looking contemplative as he sits with his head in his paws, he's pondering his new fur texture, or perhaps the meaning of life or perhaps he's just wondering what's for lunch.

Humboldt . . . The Simple Bear – #227703

Louella & Hedda . . . The Secret . . . Louella has some secrets to share with her good friend Hedda and from the look on Hedda's face, those secrets are pretty juicy! Their little friend walking hand-in-hand with Hedda looks curious – maybe they're talking about what kind of presents to buy him!

Louella & Hedda . . . The Secret – #22705

Neville . . . Compubear . . . It's the computer age and with his "Micro-Bear 3000 – Six." this bear has jumped on the technological bandwagon. His mouse and debugger sit nearby – my, that looks just like a hammer! Neville is looking a bit perplexed – for some reason, his computer screen is completely blank. Could it be that the cord is in his furry companion's hand and not actually plugged in? Neville is the Bearstones first shelf sitter and is the perfect companion for any computer wiz as he has the ability to sit atop a monitor (he even comes with free double-sided tape!).

Neville . . . Compubear – #227702

Prince Hamalot . . . Faced with the eternal question, "To Diet Or Not To Diet," this royal bear has decided to let himself eat cake. His trusty sword, Excalorie, sits nearby, ready for the Battle Of The Bulge. Dressed in purple robes, secured by a medallion adorned with the kingdom's flatware crest, this piece, with a special bottomstamp, will be making its royal debut at dealers hosting special events from May to December 1997.

Prince Hamalot – #01997-71
Special Event Figurine

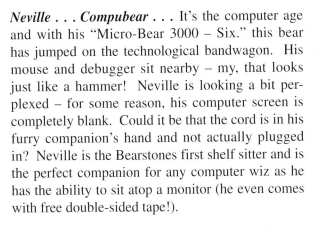

COLLECTOR'S
VALUE GUIDE™

Winkie & Dink . . . As The Lambs . . . Winkie and Dink are as cuddly as can be as new editions to the Holiday Pageant. Dressed in their finest woolens, these two little actors are ready to sit tight and watch over the Baby Jesus as he sleeps peacefully in the manger. Or maybe they're not ready for their roles just yet; didn't anyone tell them that lambs don't walk on two legs?

Winkie & Dink . . . As The
Lambs – #2409
Holiday Pageant Series

OTHER PIECES

Two new musical waterglobes have been added to the collection in 1997: the limited edition "The Flying Lesson . . . This End Up" and "Homer On The Plate," both based on resin figurines of the same name. There also are two new votives: Daphne has her carrot and gardening book and sits beside an impressive example of her gardening skills in "Daphne . . . In The Cabbage Patch," while "Ms. Bruin & Bailey . . . Tea Time" adds a touch of class as the bears enjoy their tea by the side of a dainty teacup. And in 1997, there are five new ways to wear your bears: "Bailey . . . Chocolate Wreath" for the romantic, "Bailey . . . Tea Time" for the thirsty, "Clara . . . Get Well" for those feeling under the weather, "J.B. & The Basketballs" for the sports fan and "Wilson . . . In Love" for the amorous.

The Flying Lesson
. . . This End Up
(LE-1997) – #270601

Homer On The
Plate – #270550

Daphne . . . In The
Cabbage Patch
– #27750

Ms. Bruin & Bailey
. . . Tea Time
– #27751

Bailey . . . Chocolate
Wreath – #26104

Bailey . . . Tea
Time – #26102

Clara . . . Get Well
– #26103

J.B. & The
Basketballs – #26100

Wilson . . . In Love
– #26101

COLLECTOR'S
VALUE GUIDE™

What's New

BEARSTONE EXCLUSIVE

Baby's First Christmas (ornament) . . . Among the many "new arrivals" that will be delivered in 1997, "Baby's First Christmas," an exclusive ornament in The Bearstone Collection is a special way to commemorate your "little one's" first Christmas. A Bearstone "guardian angel" sits atop the sphere and reads from his book the night-time prayer "Now I lay me down to sleep." Wrapped in a ribbon declaring "Baby's First Christmas" and decorated with hobbyhorses and snowflakes, this ball ornament would make a nice addition to your tree (to complement the new addition to your family)!

Baby's First Christmas
– #25703

The Folkstone Collection®

There are 12 new resin introduction and five new pins in the Folkstone Collection in 1997. In addition to the six conventional pieces (if you can call them conventional), Boyds introduces The Wee Folkstones, comprised of six "Not Quite Guardian Angels" to help with all of life's little problems.

FIGURINES

Angelina "Smidge" Angellove . . . Angel Of True Love . . . This little angel of love has the key to your heart – and if it doesn't fit, she has a "smidge" of "Love Potion #9" to help things along. In her pink lace dress and adorned with hearts from head to foot, Angelina is the perfect picture of true love.

Angelina "Smidge"
Angellove . . . Angel Of
True Love – #36100
The Wee Folkstones

COLLECTOR'S
VALUE GUIDE™

Constance & Felicity . . . Best Friend Angels (LE-1997) . . . These two angels stand with arms around each other, ready to share their "Book of Secrets" as they hold a token of their friendship which bears the message, "Friends." At their feet, two heavenly, furry friends sit in similar fashion, holding a banner to complete the message, "Forever." While true friendship is endless, the supply of this piece is not, as it is limited to only one year of production.

Constance & Felicity . . .
Best Friend Angels
(LE-1997) – #28205

Dentinata "Faeriefloss" . . . The Tooth Faerie . . . Losing teeth can be very profitable when this little faerie, armed with a toothbrush and wearing a crown of teeth, comes around. Leave a tooth under your pillow before you go to bed and in the morning, you just may find a shiny new quarter in its place. Looks like it's been a busy night of pillow hopping for Dentinata, judging by her full bag of baby teeth.

Dentinata "Faeriefloss"
. . . The Tooth Faerie
– #36102
The Wee Folkstones

"Electra" Angelbyte . . . Angel In Computer Training . . . Electra sits at her celestial computer, eager to try out the new programs that she has learned about in her text books. She's studying hard, reading about the Web and lots of other "techno-stuff." Her furry, angelic friend is there to offer advice but before he gets caught up in the Internet, he has to first get untangled from the computer cord!

"Electra" Angelbyte . . .
Angel Of Computer
Training – #36300
The Wee Folkstones

Estudious "Cram" Faeriebaum . . . The Study Faerie . . . It's five minutes before one a.m. and Estudious, cramming for the big exam, wishes that she'd spent more time hitting the books and less time doing other things. She has her mug filled to the brim and a jar of sugar to help keep those tired eyes open. First literature; next algebra; then . . . is it summer vacation yet?

Estudious "Cram"
Faeriebaum . . . The Study
Faerie – #36301
The Wee Folkstones

COLLECTOR'S
VALUE GUIDE™

What's New

Immaculata Faerieburg . . . The Cleaning Faerie
. . . "It's so shiny, I can see myself," Immaculata
says to herself as she scrubs, scours and shines on
her hands and knees. Dressed in an apron and pink
gloves, this faerie is armed with a bucketful of suds
and a scrub brush and looks ready to tackle any
size cleaning job.

Immaculata Faerieburg . . .
The Cleaning Faerie
– #36302
The Wee Folkstones

Infiniti Faerielove . . . The Wedding Faerie . . .
You don't need to read the heart Infiniti holds in
her hand, her name says it all – love is forever.
Wearing a crown of pink roses (the flowers of
love), Infiniti is designed to sit on a shelf, perhaps
beside a memento of your very own special day.

Infiniti Faerielove . . . The
Wedding Faerie – #36101
The Wee Folkstones

Mercy . . . Angel of Nurses . . . This would-be
Florence Nightingale knows that a little bit of sugar
makes the medicine go down, so she's brought a
big jar of honey to her ailing patients. Mercy's
actions are full of love, embodied in the hearts on
her hat, lapel and apron.

Mercy . . . Angel Of
Nurses – #28240

Ms. Patience . . . Angel of Teachers . . . Standing
on a pedestal that reads "There is no such thing as a
foolish question" and understanding the value of a
little time and patience, this schoolmistress is ready
to take a break from her busy teaching schedule to
help students. And on top of that, she is completely prepared for class with her ruler in her pocket,
texts in her hand and bell to let students know that
class is about to begin. This teacher really has her
hands full – maybe too full as she has dropped a
piece of chalk which lies broken at her feet.

Ms. Patience . . . Angel Of
Teachers – #28241

COLLECTOR'S
VALUE GUIDE™

Prudence . . . Daffodils . . . Prudence has been a wise hare to wait to pick the daffodils from her garden because now they are in perfect bloom! Holding her little companion in one arm, she cradles a fresh bouquet in her apron and has gathered up just enough for herself to decorate the brim of her hat, which her floppy ears almost cover.

Prudence . . . Daffodils
– #2847

Santa's Hobby (LE-1997) . . . This enchanting limited edition was available through selected retailers in 1996 as an early release, but can now be found at general Boyds retailers. Santa looks his merry self as he puts the final stitches into a well-stuffed teddy. All his materials lie close at hand, including a measuring tape and a box of button eyes. This piece will be the last in the *Santa & Friends* series, which concludes this year.

Santa's Hobby (LE-1997)
– #3004
Santa & Friends

Sgt. Rex & Matt . . . The Runaway . . . This little teddy's adventure was cut short when canine Sgt. Rex sniffed him out him walking along the avenue with his belongings wrapped tightly in a scarf and tied on a stick. As Rex takes Matt by the hand and gets ready to bring this would-be explorer home, this little Lewis and Clark wanna-be looks up at him, begging to let him resume his journey.

Sgt. Rex & Matt . . .
The Runaway – #2874

Ziggy . . . The Duffer . . . Ziggy may look spiffy in his argyle sweater and matching hat, but his actual game isn't as up to par. At least this moose is well prepared for his mishaps; he has a whole bucket full of golf balls for those shots that go awry. And being particularly fond of water plants, this golfer doesn't mind having to search for a stray shot in the water hazards – any opportunity for a mid-game snack is all right with him!

Ziggy . . . The Duffer
– #2838

What's New

OTHER PIECES

Nothing makes a fashion statement quite like wearing a Folkstone pin on your lapel! There are five new Folkwear pieces in 1997: "Baby Amelia's Carrot Juice," "Betty Biscuit" and "Eloise . . . Tea Toter" make refreshing fashion accessories; "Florina's Wreath" expresses a flowery greeting; and "Ms. Patience . . . The Teacher" makes the perfect gift for that special instructor.

| Baby Amelia's Carrot Juice – #26404 | Betty Biscuit – #26403 | Eloise . . . Tea Toter – #26402 | Florina's Wreath – #26400 | Ms. Patience . . . The Teacher – #26401 |

THE DOLLSTONE COLLECTION ™

There are six resin figurines and one candle votive new to the Dollstone family for 1997. This year's introductions bring a very special look of innocence to the collection with their wide, imploring eyes.

FIGURINES

The Amazing Bailey . . . "Magic Show At 4" (LE-1997) . . . The stage is set and Bailey is getting ready to perform her sleight-of-hand magic tricks for the audience of dolls and furry friends who have gathered around. Her many assistants patiently await their roles in the show and their chances for fame. For her first trick, Bailey will pull a rabbit from a hat (although he looks quite comfortable lounging on top) and then, she'll dazzle the audience by sawing a bear in half!

The Amazing Bailey . . . "Magic Show At 4" (LE-1997) – #3518

Julia With Emmy Lou & Daphne . . . Garden Friends . . . Decked out in a flowered gardening hat, Julia reads up on her gardening tips with two trusty helpers by her side. Tokens of gardening such as carrot buttons on Julia's dress and a large watering can in Emmy Lou's paws show how determined these gardeners are.

Julia With Emmy Lou & Daphne . . . Garden Friends – #3520

Laura With Jane . . . First Day Of School . . . Everyone knows that the first day of school can be scary and although Laura is trying very hard to be brave, the tear rolling down her cheek betrays her efforts. Dressed in her brand new school dress, Laura is well-prepared for class with her text books and lunch box. Her doll friend, Jane, has come along for the walk and holds a shiny red apple that Laura will give to her new teacher.

Laura With Jane . . . First Day Of School – #3522

Natalie With Joy . . . Sunday School . . . Natalie and Joy are very special additions to The Dollstone Collection not only because of their beauty but also because they are the first African-American characters to be introduced into The Dollstone Collection. Walking hand-in-hand on a rocky road lined with blooming flowers, these two girls enjoy a beautiful Sunday morning stroll to the church.

Natalie With Joy . . . Sunday School – #3519

Wendy With Bronte, Keats, Tennyson & Poe . . . Wash Day . . . Wendy was very serious when she promised mom that she'd take care of the four stray cats if she were allowed to keep them. Once a week, she helps them into a giant washtub and scrubs them until their fur is nice and shiny – nothing but the best for tabbies who are named after literary greats! The kittens don't seem to be enjoying the bath, but perhaps the towel massage might make it all worth it!

Wendy With Bronte, Keats, Tennyson & Poe . . . Wash Day – #3521

COLLECTOR'S
VALUE GUIDE™

What's New

Whitney With Wilson . . . Tea Party . . . Whitney has brought out the finest china and has put on her best Sunday dress and jeweled brooch. She has also picked the perfect hat for the occasion as the flowers decorating the brim match the flowers on the china. Always the perfect hostess, Whitney has made sure that her furry companion, Wilson, is made comfortable with a bib, soft blanket and a full cup of tea (a drop of which sits perched on the tip of the teapot's spout, ready to fall).

Whitney With Wilson . . .
Tea Party – #3523

OTHER PIECES

Whitney With Wilson . . . Tea And Candlelight . . . Based on "Whitney With Wilson . . . Tea Party," this teapot votive is a beautiful way to display candles. Blue, yellow and pink roses add a sense of elegance to the teapot. A drop of tea hanging from the spout and the well-worn condition of the porcelain suggest that this teapot has seen much use over the years.

Whitney With Wilson . . .
Tea And Candlelight
– #27950

THE SHOE BOX BEARS™

There's another new addition to the Shoe Box Bear family for 1997 – a daughter affectionately known as "The Goil" – plus an exclusive figurine available at selected retailers.

FIGURINES

Maisey . . . "The Goil" Grizberg . . . There's a new big sister in the poseable Shoe Box Bear family and she's quite the "goil" (hubba, hubba)! A fine sight in her pink polka-dot bow and lace ribbon, Maisey is the reigning beauty in bear social circles.

Maisey "The Goil" Grizberg
– #3203

COLLECTOR'S
VALUE GUIDE™

SHOE BOX BEARS EXCLUSIVE

Santa Shoe Box Bear . . . It's a good thing this Santa figurine is also a Shoe Box Bear – it would be tough for him to get down the chimney if his arms and legs didn't move! This colorful Santa bear is dressed for the Christmas season in a green suit and red hat and will be available only at selected retailers in 1997.

Santa Shoe Box Bear
– #3204-01

What's New

Use this section to record information about new releases, purchases you want to make or information about your favorite retailers and upcoming events.

Future Retirements – Figurines

Boyds Bears retirements are usually announced in *The Boyds Bear Retail Inquirer*. The pieces listed below will be retired by December 31, 1997, except for the ones marked with an asterisk (*) which faced "sudden death retirement" on February 21, 1997. Some of these retired pieces will be unavailable before the end of the year depending on when the stock is depleted at The Boyds Collection Ltd. The issue year and stock number are in parentheses. Do you have these soon-to-be retired pieces yet? Check with your retailer about their availability.

Retiring in 1997 . . .

The Bearstone Collection

- ❏ Bailey . . . Poor Ol' Bear (1997, #227704) *
- ❏ Celeste . . . The Angel Rabbit (1994, #2230) *
- ❏ Cookie Catberg . . . Knittin' Kitten (1995, #2250)
- ❏ Elgin The Elf Bear (1994, #2236) *
- ❏ The Flying Lesson . . . This End Up (LE-1997, #227801)
- ❏ Knute & The Gridiron (1994, #2245) *
- ❏ Maynard The Santa Moose (1994, #2238) *
- ❏ Otis . . . Tax Time (1995, #2262) *
- ❏ Prince Hamalot (1997, #01997-71)
- ❏ Ted & Teddy (1994, #2223)
- ❏ Wilson At The Beach (1994, #2020-06)
- ❏ Wilson The "Perfesser" (1994, #2222)
- ❏ Wilson With Love Sonnets (1993, #2007)
- ❏ The Flying Lesson . . . This End Up (waterglobe, LE-1997, #270601)
- ❏ Amelia (pin, 1995, #2612)
- ❏ Angelica's Flight (pin, 1994, #2605)
- ❏ Bailey's Springtime (pin, 1995, #2617)
- ❏ Daphne With Dove (pin, 1995, #2611)
- ❏ Justina, Bailey & M. Harrison (pin, 1995, #2619)

The Folkstone Collection

- ❏ Alvin T. MacBarker . . . Dog Face (1996, #2872)
- ❏ Angel Of Peace (1994, #2822)
- ❏ Constance & Felicity . . . Best Friend Angels (LE-1997, #28205)
- ❏ December 26th (1996, #3003)
- ❏ Elmo "Tex" Beefcake . . . On The Range (1996, #2853)
- ❏ Jill . . . Language Of Love (1995, #2842)
- ❏ Minerva . . . The Baseball Angel (1995, #2826)
- ❏ Nick On Ice (1994, #3001)
- ❏ Peter . . . The Whopper (1995, #2841)
- ❏ Santa's Challenge (1994, #3002)
- ❏ Santa's Flight Plan (1994, #3000)
- ❏ Santa's Hobby . . . The Teddy Bear Maker (1996, #3004)
- ❏ Alice & Emily (pin, 1996, #2666)
- ❏ Daphne In Straw Hat (pin, 1996, #2668)
- ❏ Florence Wings It (pin, 1995, #2625)
- ❏ Oceania (pin, 1996, #2674)
- ❏ Ralph Angel Pooch (pin, 1996, #2669)

The Dollstone Collection

- ❏ The Amazing Bailey . . . "Magic Show At 4" (LE-1997, #3518)

Bearfinder – Numerical Figurine Index

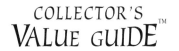

COLLECTOR'S
VALUE GUIDE™

Bearfinder – Numerical Figurine Index

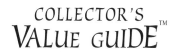

COLLECTOR'S
VALUE GUIDE™

Bearfinder – Numerical Figurine Index

COLLECTOR'S
VALUE GUIDE™

Bearfinder – Numerical Figurine Index

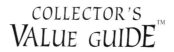

COLLECTOR'S
VALUE GUIDE™

Value Guide – Boyds Figurines

How To Use Your Value Guide

This section spotlights The Bearstone Collection, The Folkstone Collection, The Dollstone Collection, The Shoe Box Bears and Collector's Club Pieces. The pieces are listed alphabetically within each collection, with figurines listed first, followed by ornaments, waterglobes, votives and pins. If you know only the item numbers of your pieces instead of the names, refer to the *Bearfinder – Numerical Figurine Index* on page 24 to find their location in the value guide.

How To Total The Value Of Your Collection

Totaling the value of your collection is as easy as 1-2-3. Simply follow the steps below and see how easy it can be!

1. Look at the bottom of your piece to determine the edition number (see *Secondary Market Overview* for more on edition numbers).

2. Refer to the market values as listed in the picture boxes. Market values are listed for 1E's, a price range is listed for 2E's and 3E's and the "All Ed." value is the current market value for "all editions" numbered 4E and higher. For current pieces, the "All Ed." value will be listed as the approximate current retail price. For pieces that do not have editions (such as ornaments and pins), there will be only one market value listed. If a price is listed as "*N/A*," an edition number does not exist for the piece. For more information on pieces with variations, see the *Variations* section on page 129.

3. You can then total the columns at the bottom of the page (use a pencil so you can change totals as your collection grows) and transfer each subtotal to the summary page at the end of the section to come up with the total value of your collection.

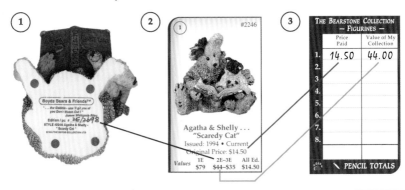

THE BEARSTONE COLLECTION

1 #2246

**Agatha & Shelly . . .
"Scaredy Cat"**
Issued: 1994 • Current
Original Price: $14.50

Values	1E	2E-3E	All Ed.
	$79	$44–$35	$14.50

2 #2258

**Amelia's Enterprise . . .
Carrot Juice**
Issued: 1995 • Current
Original Price: $16.50

Values	1E	2E-3E	All Ed.
	$73	$33–$28	$16.50

3 #2266

Angelica . . . The Guardian
Issued: 1995 • Current
Original Price: $18.50

Values	1E	2E-3E	All Ed.
	$62	$36–$28	$18.50

4 #2411

NEW!

**Ariel & Clarence . . . As
The Pair O'Angels**
Holiday Pageant Series
Issued: 1997 • Current
Original Price: $15.00

Values	1E	2E-3E	All Ed.
	$15	$15–$15	$15

5 #2003-03

Arthur . . . With Red Scarf
Issued: 1993 • Retired: 1994
Original Price: $11.00

Values	1E	2E-3E	All Ed.
	$130	$84–$60	$44

6 #2018

**Bailey & Emily . . .
Forever Friends**
Issued: 1994 • Retired: 1996
Original Price: $34.00

Values	1E	2E-3E	All Ed.
	$130	$78–$69	$48

7 #2017

**Bailey & Wixie . . .
To Have And To Hold**
Issued: 1994 • Current
Original Price: $16.00

Values	1E	2E-3E	All Ed.
	$280	$120–$105	$16

8 #2020-09

Bailey At The Beach
Issued: 1994 • Retired: 1995
Original Price: $16.00

Values	1E	2E-3E	All Ed.
	$147	$96–$79	$48

**THE BEARSTONE COLLECTION
— FIGURINES —**

	Price Paid	Value of My Collection
1.		
2.		
3.		
4.		
5.		
6.		
7.		
8.		

 ＼ PENCIL TOTALS

1   #2000

Variation

Bailey Bear With Suitcase
Issued: 1993 • Current
Original Price: $14.50

Values	1E	2E-3E	All Ed.
	$395	$255–$200	$14.50

Variation: smooth fur, brown bottom

Values	1E	2E-3E	All Ed.
	$104	N/A	N/A

---

2   #2272

Bailey ... Heart's Desire
Issued: 1996 • Current
Original Price: $15.00

Values	1E	2E-3E	All Ed.
	$98	$50–$37	$15

---

3   #2006

Bailey ... In The Orchard
Issued: 1993 • Retired: 1996
Original Price: $14.50

Values	1E	2E-3E	All Ed.
	N/A	N/A	$30

Variation: paw print on jug

Values	1E	2E-3E	All Ed.
	$210	$105–$95	$50

---

4   #227704

NEW!

Bailey ... Poor Ol' Bear
Issued: 1997 • Retired: 1997
Original Price: $15.00

Values	1E	2E-3E	All Ed.
	N/E	N/E	N/E

N/E – Values not established

---

5   #2254

Variation

Bailey The Baker ... With Sweetie Pie
Issued: 1995 • Current
Original Price: $13.00

Values	1E	2E-3E	All Ed.
	$90	$42–$35	$13

Variation: "Clarion Bear," available 6/95 at Teddy Bear Festival in Clarion, Iowa

Values	1E	2E-3E	All Ed.
	$240	N/A	N/A

---

6   #2268

Bailey ... The Cheerleader
Issued: 1995 • Current
Original Price: $16.00

Values	1E	2E-3E	All Ed.
	$56	$42–$28	$16

THE BEARSTONE COLLECTION – FIGURINES –

	Price Paid	Value of My Collection
1.		
2.		
3.		
4.		
5.		
6.		
7.		
8.		

PENCIL TOTALS

---

7   #227701-10

NEW!

Bailey ... The Graduate – Carpe Diem
Issued: 1997 • Current
Original Price: $17.00

Values	1E	2E-3E	All Ed.
	$17	$17–$17	$17

---

8   #2260

Bailey ... The Honey Bear
Issued: 1995 • Current
Original Price: $16.00

Values	1E	2E-3E	All Ed.
	$82	$48–$30	$16

1 #2014

Bailey's Birthday
Issued: 1994 • Current
Original Price: $16.00

Values	1E	2E–3E	All Ed.
	$190	$100–$75	$16

2 #2403

Baldwin . . . As The Child
Holiday Pageant Series
Issued: 1995 • Current
Original Price: $15.00

Values	1E	2E–3E	All Ed.
	$40	$25–$18	$15

3 #2239

Bessie The Santa Cow
Issued: 1994 • Retired: 1996
Original Price: $16.00

Values	1E	2E–3E	All Ed.
	$83	$52–$40	$30

4 #2410

NEW!

Bruce . . . As The Shepherd
Holiday Pageant Series
Issued: 1997 • Current
Original Price: $15.00

Values	1E	2E–3E	All Ed.
	$15	$15–$15	$15

5 #227706

NEW!

Buzz . . . The Flash
Issued: 1997 • Current
Original Price: $18.00

Values	1E	2E–3E	All Ed.
	$18	$18–$18	$18

6 #2010

**Byron & Chedda
With Catmint**
Issued: 1993 • Retired: 1994
Original Price: $14.50

Values	1E	2E–3E	All Ed.
	N/A	N/A–$73	$50

Variation: no patches on left arm

Values	1E	2E–3E	All Ed.
	$125	$92–$75	N/A

7 #2230

**Celeste . . . The
Angel Rabbit**
Issued: 1994 • Retired: 1997
Original Price: $16.50

Values	1E	2E–3E	All Ed.
	$300	$183–$130	$33

8 #2229

**Charlotte & Bebe . . .
The Gardeners**
Issued: 1994 • Retired: 1995
Original Price: $16.00

Values	1E	2E–3E	All Ed.
	$105	$71–$55	$40

**THE BEARSTONE COLLECTION
— FIGURINES —**

	Price Paid	Value of My Collection
1.		
2.		
3.		
4.		
5.		
6.		
7.		
8.		

PENCIL TOTALS

① #2012

Christian By The Sea
Issued: 1993 • Current
Original Price: $14.50

Values	1E	2E–3E	All Ed.
	$118	$67–$52	$14.50

② #2231

Clara . . . The Nurse (RS)
Issued: 1994 • Current
Original Price: $16.00

Values	1E	2E–3E	All Ed.
	N/A	*N/A*	$16

Variation: Original Version

Values	1E	2E–3E	All Ed.
	$340	$195–$158	$16

③ #2029-11

Clarence Angel Bear
Issued: 1994 • Retired: 1995
Original Price: $13.00

Values	1E	2E–3E	All Ed.
	$120	$72–$50	$35

④ #2250

**Cookie Catberg . . .
Knittin' Kitten**
Issued: 1995 • Current
Original Price: $19.00

Values	1E	2E–3E	All Ed.
	$68	$47–$32	$19

⑤ #2237

Cookie The Santa Cat
Issued: 1994 • Retired: 1995
Original Price: $15.50

Values	1E	2E–3E	All Ed.
	$86	$54–$41	$34

⑥ #2251

**Daphne & Eloise . . .
Women's Work**
Issued: 1995 • Current
Original Price: $18.00

Values	1E	2E–3E	All Ed.
	$72	$40–$32	$18

**THE BEARSTONE COLLECTION
– FIGURINES –**

	Price Paid	Value of My Collection
1.		
2.	✓	
3.		
4.		
5.		
6.		
7.		
8.		

PENCIL TOTALS

⑦ #2011

**Daphne Hare &
Maisey Ewe**
Issued: 1993 • Retired: 1995
Original Price: $14.50

Values	1E	2E–3E	All Ed.
	$124	$78–$60	$44

⑧ #2226

**Daphne . . . The
Reader Hare**
Issued: 1994 • Current
Original Price: $14.50

Values	1E	2E–3E	All Ed.
	$120	$73–$54	$14.50

THE BEARSTONE COLLECTION

1 #2240

**Edmund & Bailey . . .
Gathering Holly**
Issued: 1994 • Current
Original Price: $24.00

Values	1E	2E–3E	All Ed.
	$162	$77–$50	$24

2 NEW! #227701-07

**Edmund . . . The Graduate
– Carpe Diem**
Issued: 1997 • Current
Original Price: $17.00

Values	1E	2E–3E	All Ed.
	$17	$17–$17	$17

3 #2236

Elgin The Elf Bear
Issued: 1994 • Retired: 1997
Original Price: $14.50

Values	1E	2E–3E	All Ed.
	$85	$54–$41	$14.50

4 #2242

Elliot & Snowbeary
Issued: 1994 • Current
Original Price: $15.50

Values	1E	2E–3E	All Ed.
	$100	$63–$42	$15.50

5 #2241

Elliot & The Tree
Issued: 1994 • Current
Original Price: $16.50

Values	1E	2E–3E	All Ed.
	$184	$110–$70	$16.50

6 #2280

Elliot . . . The Hero
Issued: 1996 • Current
Original Price: $17.00

Values	1E	2E–3E	All Ed.
	$60	$42–$27	$17

7 #2277

**Emma & Bailey . . .
Afternoon Tea**
Issued: 1996 • Current
Original Price: $18.00

Values	1E	2E–3E	All Ed.
	$78	$50–$39	$18

8 #2269

Emma . . . The Witchy Bear
Issued: 1995 • Current
Original Price: $17.50

Values	1E	2E–3E	All Ed.
	$67	$43–$36	$17.50

**THE BEARSTONE COLLECTION
– FIGURINES –**

	Price Paid	Value of My Collection
1.		
2.		
3.		
4.		
5.	✓	
6.		
7.		
8.		

PENCIL TOTALS

(1) #2408

NEW!

Essex . . . As The Donkey
Holiday Pageant Series
Issued: 1997 • Current
Original Price: $15.00

Values	1E	2E–3E	All Ed.
	$15	$15–$15	$15

(2) #2008

Father Chrisbear And Son
Issued: 1993 • Retired: 1993
Original Price: $14.50

Values	1E	2E–3E	All Ed.
	$365	N/A	N/A

(3) #227801

NEW!

The Flying Lesson . . . This End Up (LE-1997)
Issued: 1997 • Current
Original Price: $63.00

Values	Jan	Feb–Mar	Apr–Dec
	$63	$63–$63	$63

(4) #2016

Variation

Grenville & Beatrice . . . Best Friends
Issued: 1994 • Current
Original Price: $26.00

Values	1E	2E–3E	All Ed.
	N/A	$102–$80	$26

Variation: dove on right front stones

Values	1E	2E–3E	All Ed.
	$355	N/A	N/A

(5) #2274

Grenville & Beatrice . . . True Love
Issued: 1996 • Current
Original Price: $37.00

Values	1E	2E–3E	All Ed.
	$98	$68–$53	$37

(6) #2255

Grenville & Knute . . . Football Buddies
Issued: 1995 • Current
Original Price: $20.00

Values	1E	2E–3E	All Ed.
	$67	$42–$33	$20

THE BEARSTONE COLLECTION – FIGURINES –

	Price Paid	Value of My Collection
1.		
2.		
3.		
4.		
5.		
6.		
7. ✓		
8.		

PENCIL TOTALS

(7) #2099

Grenville & Neville . . . The Sign
Issued: 1993 • Current
Original Price: $16.00

Values	White Bottom:	$16
	Brown Bottom:	$135

(8) #2233

Grenville . . . The Graduate
Issued: 1994 • Retired: 1996
Original Price: $16.50

Values	1E	2E–3E	All Ed.
	$112	$74–$68	$45

THE BEARSTONE COLLECTION

1 #2030

Grenville The Santabear
Issued: 1994 • Retired: 1996
Original Price: $14.50

Values	1E	2E–3E	All Ed.
	$520	$300–$240	$65

2 #2265

Grenville . . . The Storyteller (LE-1995)
Issued: 1995 • Retired: 1995
Original Price: $47.00

Values	Jan	Feb–Mar	Apr–Dec
	$140	$85–$70	$55

3 #2003-04

Grenville . . . With Green Scarf
Issued: 1993 • Retired: 1993
Original Price: $11.00

Values	1E	2E–3E	All Ed.
	$410	$350–N/A	N/A

4 #2281

Grenville With Matthew & Bailey . . . Sunday Afternoon
Issued: 1996 • Current
Original Price: $36.00

Values	1E	2E–3E	All Ed.
	$70	$46–$36	$36

5 #2003-08

Grenville . . . With Red Scarf (RS)
Issued: 1993 • Retired: 1995
Original Price: $11.00

Values	1E	2E–3E	All Ed.
	N/A	N/A	$48

Variation: Original Version

Values	1E	2E–3E	All Ed.
	$144	$73–$64	$48

6 #2405

Heath . . . As Caspar
Holiday Pageant Series
Issued: 1996 • Current
Original Price: $15.00

Values	1E	2E–3E	All Ed.
	$36	$28–$15	$15

7 #2225

Homer On The Plate
Issued: 1994 • Current
Original Price: $16.00

Values	1E	2E–3E	All Ed.
	$94	$48–$35	$16

8 #2247

Hop-A-Long . . . The Deputy
Issued: 1995 • Current
Original Price: $14.00

Values	1E	2E–3E	All Ed.
	$58	$40–$28	$14

THE BEARSTONE COLLECTION – FIGURINES –

	Price Paid	Value of My Collection
1.	✓	
2.		
3.		
4.		
5.		
6.		
7.		
8.		

PENCIL TOTALS

1 NEW! #227703

Humboldt . . . The Simple Bear
Issued: 1997 • Current
Original Price: $12.00

Values	1E	2E–3E	All Ed.
	$12	$12–$12	$12

2 #2029-10

Juliette Angel Bear
Issued: 1994 • Retired: 1995
Original Price: $13.00

Values	1E	2E–3E	All Ed.
	$108	$63–$50	$35

3 #2015

Justina & M. Harrison . . . Sweetie Pie
Issued: 1994 • Current
Original Price: $26.00

Values	1E	2E–3E	All Ed.
	$98	$56–$43	$26

4 #2273

Justina . . . The Message "Bearer"
Issued: 1996 • Current
Original Price: $16.00

Values	1E	2E–3E	All Ed.
	$55	$32–$28	$16

5 #2245

Knute & The Gridiron
Issued: 1994 • Retired: 1997
Original Price: $16.50

Values	1E	2E–3E	All Ed.
	$77	$50–$33	$24

6 #2235

Kringle & Bailey With List
Issued: 1994 • Current
Original Price: $14.50

Values	1E	2E–3E	All Ed.
	$89	$55–$32	$14.50

THE BEARSTONE COLLECTION – FIGURINES –

	Price Paid	Value of My Collection
1.		
2.		
3.		
4.	✓	
5.		
6.		
7.	✓	
8.		

🐾 \ **PENCIL TOTALS**

7 #2283

Kringle And Company
Issued: 1996 • Current
Original Price: $18.00

Values	1E	2E–3E	All Ed.
	$56	$34–$25	$18

8 #2283-01

Kringle And Company (GCC Exclusive)
Issued: 1996 • Retired: 1996
Original Price: $18.00

Values	1E	2E–3E	All Ed.
	$95	$43–$38	$30

1 #2253

Lefty On The Mound
Issued: 1995 • Current
Original Price: $15.00

Values	1E	2E–3E	All Ed.
	$85	$45–$34	$15

2 #227705

NEW!

**Louella & Hedda . . .
The Secret**
Issued: 1997 • Current
Original Price: $19.00

Values	1E	2E–3E	All Ed.
	$19	$19–$19	$19

3 #2275

M. Harrison's Birthday
Issued: 1996 • Current
Original Price: $17.00

Values	1E	2E–3E	All Ed.
	$58	$37–$25	$17

4 #2243

Manheim The Eco-Moose
Issued: 1994 • Current
Original Price: $15.50

Values	1E	2E–3E	All Ed.
	$75	$38–$32	$15.50

5 #2285V

picture
not
available

**Margot (QVC Exclusive,
Premier Edition only)**
Issued: 1997 • Sold Out: 1997
Original Price: $18.00
Value $40

6 #2238

**Maynard The Santa
Moose**
Issued: 1994 • Retired: 1997
Original Price: $15.50

Values	1E	2E–3E	All Ed.
	$86	$48–$39	$15.50

7 #2282

**Momma McBear . . .
Anticipation**
Issued: 1996 • Current
Original Price: $15.00

Values	1E	2E–3E	All Ed.
	$60	$35–$26	$15

8 #2005

**Moriarty - The Bear In
The Cat Suit**
Issued: 1993 • Retired: 1995
Original Price: $14.00

Values	1E	2E–3E	All Ed.
	N/A	N/A	$46

Variation: 1993 on side of base

Values	1E	2E–3E	All Ed.
	$132	$79–$67	$46

**THE BEARSTONE COLLECTION
– FIGURINES –**

| | Price
Paid | Value of My
Collection |
|---|---|---|
| 1. | | |
| 2. | | |
| 3. | | |
| 4. | | |
| 5. | | |
| 6. | | |
| 7. | | |
| 8. | | |

PENCIL TOTALS

1 #2259

**Ms. Bruin & Bailey ...
The Lesson**
Issued: 1995 • Current
Original Price: $18.50

Values	1E	2E–3E	All Ed.
	$130	$58–$37	$18.50

2 #2276

Variation

**Ms. Griz ... Monday
Morning**
Issued: 1996 • Current
Original Price: $35.00

Values	1E	2E–3E	All Ed.
	$88	$45–$35	$35

Variation: pink dress

Values	1E	2E–3E	All Ed.
	$100	$85–$58	$46

3 #2284

**Ms. Griz ... Saturday
Night (GCC Exclusive)**
Issued: 1996 • Retired: 1996
Original Price: $15.00

Values	1E	2E–3E	All Ed.
	$66	$52–$42	$35

4 #2401

Neville ... As Joseph
Holiday Pageant Series
Issued: 1995 • Current
Original Price: $15.00

Values	1E	2E–3E	All Ed.
	$40	$27–$15	$15

5 #227702

NEW!

Neville ... Compubear
Issued: 1997 • Current
Original Price: $16.50

Values	1E	2E–3E	All Ed.
	$16.50	$16.50	$16.50

6 #2002

**Neville ... The
Bedtime Bear**
Issued: 1993 • Retired: 1996
Original Price: $14.50

Values	1E	2E–3E	All Ed.
	$128	$84–$75	$44

**THE BEARSTONE COLLECTION
– FIGURINES –**

	Price Paid	Value of My Collection
1.		
2.		
3.		
4.		
5.		
6.		
7.		
8.		

\ **PENCIL TOTALS**

7 #2278

**Noah & Co ... Ark
Builders (LE-1996)**
Issued: 1996 • Retired: 1996
Original Price: $63.00

Values	Jan	Feb–Mar	Apr–Dec
	$135	$106–$88	$80

8 #2262

Otis ... Tax Time
Issued: 1995 • Retired: 1997
Original Price: $19.00

Values	1E	2E–3E	All Ed.
	$74	$49–$40	$28

1 #2249-06

Otis . . . The Fisherman
Issued: 1995 • Current
Original Price: $16.00

Values	1E	2E–3E	All Ed.
	$69	$45–$31	$16

2 #01997-71

NEW!

Prince Hamalot (Special Event Piece, LE-1997)
Issued: 1997 • Current
Original Price: $30.00
Value $30

3 #2406

Raleigh . . . As Balthasar
Holiday Pageant Series
Issued: 1996 • Current
Original Price: $15.00

Values	1E	2E–3E	All Ed.
	$40	$28–$15	$15

4 #2227

Sebastian's Prayer
Issued: 1994 • Retired: 1996
Original Price: $16.50

Values	1E	2E–3E	All Ed.
	$92	$67–$54	$40

5 #2019

Sherlock & Watson . . . In Disguise
Issued: 1994 • Retired: 1996
Original Price: $16.00

Values	1E	2E–3E	All Ed.
	$128	$70–$48	$33

6 #2267

Simone & Bailey . . . Helping Hands
Issued: 1995 • Current
Original Price: $26.00

Values	1E	2E–3E	All Ed.
	$63	$44–$35	$26

7 #2001

Variation

A MOTHER'S LOVE

Simone de Bearvoire & Her Mom, My Auntie Alice
Issued: 1993 • Retired: 1996
Original Price: $14.50

Values	1E	2E–3E	All Ed.
	N/A	N/A	$35

Variation: no patches on paws

Values	1E	2E–3E	All Ed.
	$330	$192–$145	$103

8 #2279

Sir Edmund . . . Persistence
Issued: 1996 • Current
Original Price: $21.00

Values	1E	2E–3E	All Ed.
	$72	$41–$30	$21

THE BEARSTONE COLLECTION – FIGURINES –

	Price Paid	Value of My Collection
1.		
2.		
3.		
4.		
5.		
6.		
7.		
8.		

PENCIL TOTALS

1   #2425

The Stage . . .
School Pageant
Holiday Pageant Series
Issued: 1995 • Current
Original Price: $35.00

Values	1E	2E–3E	All Ed.
	$42	$35–$35	$35

2   #2223

Ted & Teddy
Issued: 1994 • Current
Original Price: $16.00

Values	1E	2E–3E	All Ed.
	$133	$64–$40	$16

3   #2407

Thatcher & Eden . . .
As The Camel
Issued: 1996 • Current
Original Price: $18.00

Values	1E	2E–3E	All Ed.
	$32	$25–$18	$18

4   #2402

Theresa . . . As Mary
Holiday Pageant Series
Issued: 1995 • Current
Original Price: $15.00

Values	1E	2E–3E	All Ed.
	$37	$25–$15	$15

5   #2263

Union Jack . . .
Love Letters
Issued: 1995 • Current
Original Price: $19.00

Values	1E	2E–3E	All Ed.
	$70	$43–$36	$19

6   #2004

Victoria . . . The Lady
Issued: 1993 • Current
Original Price: $18.50

Values	1E	2E–3E	All Ed.
	$240	$190–$137	$18.50

THE BEARSTONE COLLECTION
– FIGURINES –

	Price Paid	Value of My Collection
1.		
2.		
3.		
4.		
5.		
6.		
7.		
8.		

PENCIL TOTALS

7   #2404

Wilson . . . As Melchior
Holiday Pageant Series
Issued: 1996 • Current
Original Price: $15.00

Values	1E	2E–3E	All Ed.
	$33	$24–$15	$15

8   #2020-06

Wilson At The Beach
Issued: 1994 • Current
Original Price: $16.00

Values	1E	2E–3E	All Ed.
	$130	$65–$48	$16

1 #2222

Wilson The Perfesser
Issued: 1994 • Current
Original Price: $16.50

Values	1E	2E–3E	All Ed.
	$98	$65–$40	$16.50

2 #2261

Wilson . . . The Wonderful Wizard Of Wuz
Issued: 1995 • Current
Original Price: $16.50

Values	1E	2E–3E	All Ed.
	$61	$43–$29	$16.50

3 #2007

Wilson With Love Sonnets
Issued: 1993 • Current
Original Price: $13.00

Values	1E	2E–3E	All Ed.
	$520	$380–$245	$13

4 #2409

NEW!

Winkie & Dink . . . As The Lambs
Holiday Pageant Series
Issued: 1997 • Current
Original Price: $12.00

Values	1E	2E–3E	All Ed.
	$12	$12–$12	$12

5 #2286

NEW!

picture
not
available

**Zoe
(GCC Exclusive)**
Issued: 1997 • Current
Original Price: N/A

Values	1E	2E–3E	All Ed.
	N/A	N/A	N/A

6 #BC22851

NEW!

Chelsea Kainada . . . The Practice (LE-1997)
Issued: 1997 • Current
Original Price: $29.99 (Canadian)

Values (U.S.)	1E	2E–3E	All Ed.
	$35	$35–$35	$35

7 #BC2051

Christmas Bear Elf With List (LE-1,872)
Issued: 1994 • Retired: 1994
Original Price: $24.99 (Canadian)
Value (U.S.) **$580**

8 #BC2228

Ewell & Walton . . . Manitoba Mooselmen (LE-12,000)
Issued: 1996 • Retired: 1996
Original Price: $24.99 (Canadian)
Value (U.S.) **$62**

THE BEARSTONE COLLECTION — FIGURINES —		
	Price Paid	Value of My Collection
1.		
2.		
3. ✓		
4.		
5.		
— CANADIAN FIGURINES —		
6.		
7.		
8.		

 \ **PENCIL TOTALS**

① #BC2210

Homer On The Plate
Issued: 1994 • Current
Original Price: $24.99 (Canadian)

Values (U.S.)	1E	2E–3E	All Ed.
	$97	$53–$40	$30

② #BC2056

Lefty On The Mound
Issued: 1994 • Current
Original Price: $24.99 (Canadian)

Values (U.S.)	1E	2E–3E	All Ed.
	$85	$49–$34	$30

③ #BC2050

Lucy Big Pig, Little Pig
Issued: 1994 • Retired: 1996
Original Price: $24.99 (Canadian)

Values (U.S.)	1E	2E–3E	All Ed.
	$130	$96–$70	$58

④ #25703

NEW!

Baby's First Christmas (NALED Exclusive)
Issued: 1997 • Current
Original Price: N/A
Value N/A

⑤ #2502

Charity . . . Angel Bear With Star
Issued: 1994 • Retired: 1996
Original Price: $10.00
Value $25

⑥ #25701

Clair With Gingerbread Man
Issued: 1996 • Current
Original Price: $11.00
Value $11

THE BEARSTONE COLLECTION — CANADIAN FIGURINES —

	Price Paid	Value of My Collection
1.		
2.		
3.		

— ORNAMENTS —

4.		
5.		
6.		
7.		
8.		

PENCIL TOTALS

⑦ #2505

Edmund . . . "Believe"
Issued: 1995 • Current
Original Price: $10.00
Value $10

⑧ #25700

Edmund With Wreath
Issued: 1996 • Current
Original Price: $11.00
Value $11

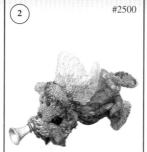

1 #2507

Elliot With Tree
Issued: 1995 • Current
Original Price: $10.00
Value **$10**

2 #2500

**Faith . . . Angel Bear
With Trumpet**
Issued: 1994 • Retired: 1996
Original Price: $10.00
Value **$25**

3 #2501

**Hope . . . Angel Bear
With Wreath**
Issued: 1994 • Retired: 1996
Original Price: $10.00
Value **$25**

4 #2506

**Manheim The Moose
With Wreath**
Issued: 1995 • Current
Original Price: $10.00
Value **$10**

5 #25702

**Wilson With
Shooting Star**
Issued: 1996 • Current
Original Price: $11.00
Value **$11**

6 #2702

Angelica . . . The Guardian
Issued: 1995 • Current
Original Price: $38.00
Value **$38**

7 #2704

Elliot And The Tree
Issued: 1995 • Current
Original Price: $36.00
Value **$36**

8 #270601

NEW!

**The Flying Lesson . . .
This End Up (LE-10,000)**
Issued: 1997 • Current
Original Price: $63.00
Value **$63**

THE BEARSTONE COLLECTION
— ORNAMENTS —

	Price Paid	Value of My Collection
1.		
2.		
3.		
4.		
5.		
— WATERGLOBES —		
6.		
7.		
8.		

\ PENCIL TOTALS

1 #2700

Grenville The Santabear
Issued: 1994 • Retired: 1996
Original Price: $36.00
Value **$60**

2 #270550

NEW!

Homer On The Plate
Issued: 1997 • Current
Original Price: $36.00
Value **$36**

3 #2706

Noah & Co. (LE-1996)
Issued: 1996 • Retired: 1996
Original Price: $53.00

Values	1E	2E–3E	All Ed.
	$195	*N/E*	*N/E*

N/E – Values not established

4 #2705

**Simone & Bailey . . .
Helping Hands**
Issued: 1996 • Current
Original Price: $36.00

Values	1E	2E–3E	All Ed.
	$36	**$36–$36**	**$36**

5 #27750

NEW!

**Daphne . . . In The
Cabbage Patch**
Issued: 1997 • Current
Original Price: $26.00

Values	1E	2E–3E	All Ed.
	$26	**$26–$26**	**$26**

6 #2772

**Edmund The Elf Bear . . .
Holiday Glow**
Issued: 1996 • Current
Original Price: $26.00

Values	1E	2E–3E	All Ed.
	$26	**$26–$26**	**$26**

**THE BEARSTONE COLLECTION
— WATERGLOBES —**

| | Price
Paid | Value of My
Collection |
|---|---|---|
| **1.** | | |
| **2.** | | |
| **3.** | | |
| **4.** | | |

— VOTIVES —

5.		
6.		
7.		
8.		

PENCIL TOTALS

7 #2771

**Elgin And Elliot The Elves
. . . Toasty Warm**
Issued: 1996 • Current
Original Price: $26.00

Values	1E	2E–3E	All Ed.
	$26	**$26–$26**	**$26**

8 #2770

**Emma The Witchy Bear
. . . Pumpkin Magic**
Issued: 1996 • Current
Original Price: $26.00

Values	1E	2E–3E	All Ed.
	$26	**$26–$26**	**$26**

1 NEW! #27751

**Ms. Bruin & Bailey . . .
Tea Time**
Issued: 1997 • Current
Original Price: $26.00

Values	1E	2E–3E	All Ed.
	$26	$26–$26	$26

2 NEW! #2258SF

Boyds Amelia's Enterprise
Issued: 1997 • Current
Original Price: $44.95

Values	1E	2E–3E	All Ed.
	$44.95	$44.95	$44.95

3 #2751

Boyds Arthur On Trunk
Issued: 1995 • Current
Original Price: $39.95

Values	1E	2E–3E	All Ed.
	$74	$45–$39.95	$39.95

*Variation: bear and trunk larger,
painted bottom, paw print on scarf*

Values	1E	2E–3E	All Ed.
	$135	N/A	N/A

4 #2018SF

Boyds Bailey & Emily
Issued: 1996 • Current
Original Price: $44.95

Values	1E	2E–3E	All Ed.
	$80	$58–$44.95	$44.95

5 #2000SF

Boyds Bailey With Suitcase
Issued: 1996 • Current
Original Price: $39.95

Values	1E	2E–3E	All Ed.
	$77	$55–$39.95	$39.95

6 #2029-11SF

Boyds Clarence Angel
Issued: 1996 • Current
Original Price: $39.95

Values	1E	2E–3E	All Ed.
	$70	$52–$39.95	$39.95

7 NEW! #2251SF

Boyds Daphne And Eloise
Issued: 1997 • Current
Original Price: $44.95

Values	1E	2E–3E	All Ed.
	$44.95	$44.95	$44.95

8 #2277SF

**Boyds Emma & Bailey
Tea Party**
Issued: 1996 • Current
Original Price: $44.95

Values	1E	2E–3E	All Ed.
	$88	$60–$44.95	$44.95

THE BEARSTONE COLLECTION
— VOTIVES —

	Price Paid	Value of My Collection
1.		

— SAN FRANCISCO MUSIC BOXES —

2.		
3.		
4.		
5.		
6.		
7.		
8.		

\ PENCIL TOTALS

---

(1) NEW! #270550SF

Boyds Homer On The Plate
Issued: 1997 • Current
Original Price: $44.95

Values	1E	2E–3E	All Ed.
	$44.95	$44.95	$44.95

---

(2) #2259SF

Boyds Miss Bruin & Bailey
Issued: 1996 • Current
Original Price: $44.95

Values	1E	2E–3E	All Ed.
	$77	$52–$44.95	$44.95

---

(3) #2002SF

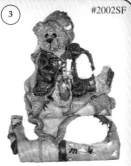

Boyds Neville Bedtime
Issued: 1996 • Current
Original Price: $39.95

Values	1E	2E–3E	All Ed.
	$75	$47–$39.95	$39.95

---

(4) #2267SF

Boyds Simone & Bailey
Issued: 1996 • Current
Original Price: $44.95

Values	1E	2E–3E	All Ed.
	$56	$49–$44.95	$44.95

---

(5) #2701

Boyds Ted & Teddy
Issued: 1995 • Current
Original Price: $39.95

Values	1E	2E–3E	All Ed.
	$74	$45–$34.95	$34.95

Variation: bears and crate slightly larger

Values	1E	2E–3E	All Ed.
	$135	N/A	N/A

---

(6) #2750

Boyds Wilson With Love Sonnets
Issued: 1995 • Current
Original Price: $39.95

Values	1E	2E–3E	All Ed.
	$75	$52–$39.95	$39.95

Variation: book base is larger, large folds in sweater

Values	1E	2E–3E	All Ed.
	$138	N/A	N/A

THE BEARSTONE COLLECTION
– SAN FRANCISCO MUSIC BOXES –

	Price Paid	Value of My Collection
1.		
2.		
3.		
4.		
5.		
6.		

– BEARWEAR PINS –

7.		
8.		

PENCIL TOTALS

---

(7) #2635

Alden & Priscilla... The Pilgrims
Issued: 1995 • Current
Original Price: $4.00
Value $4

---

(8) #2616

Alice's Flight
Issued: 1995 • Out of Production
Original Price: $4.00
Value $4

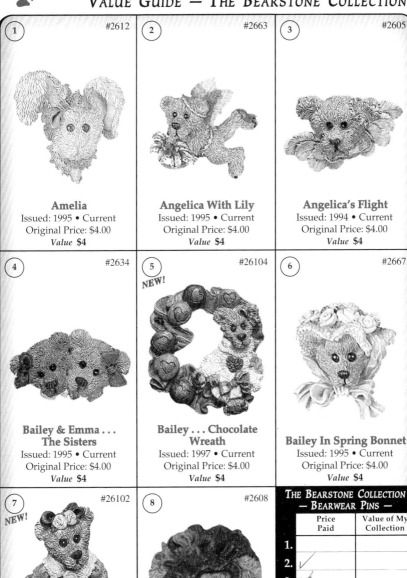

THE BEARSTONE COLLECTION

1 · #2612

Amelia
Issued: 1995 • Current
Original Price: $4.00
Value **$4**

2 · #2663

Angelica With Lily
Issued: 1995 • Current
Original Price: $4.00
Value **$4**

3 · #2605

Angelica's Flight
Issued: 1994 • Current
Original Price: $4.00
Value **$4**

4 · #2634

**Bailey & Emma...
The Sisters**
Issued: 1995 • Current
Original Price: $4.00
Value **$4**

5 · #26104 — NEW!

**Bailey ... Chocolate
Wreath**
Issued: 1997 • Current
Original Price: $4.00
Value **$4**

6 · #2667

Bailey In Spring Bonnet
Issued: 1995 • Current
Original Price: $4.00
Value **$4**

7 · #26102 — NEW!

Bailey ... Tea Time
Issued: 1997 • Current
Original Price: $4.00
Value **$4**

8 · #2608

Bailey's Bonnet
Issued: 1994 • Out of Production
Original Price: $4.00
Value **$4**

THE BEARSTONE COLLECTION
— BEARWEAR PINS —

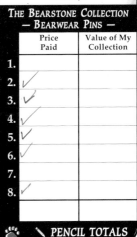

	Price Paid	Value of My Collection
1.		
2.	✓	
3.	✓	
4.	✓	
5.	✓	
6.	✓	
7.		
8.	✓	

🐾 **\ PENCIL TOTALS**

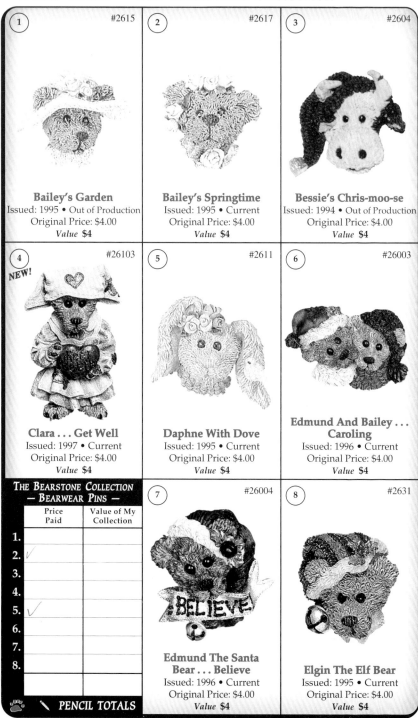

1 #2615

Bailey's Garden
Issued: 1995 • Out of Production
Original Price: $4.00
Value **$4**

2 #2617

Bailey's Springtime
Issued: 1995 • Current
Original Price: $4.00
Value **$4**

3 #2604

Bessie's Chris-moo-se
Issued: 1994 • Out of Production
Original Price: $4.00
Value **$4**

4 #26103 NEW!

Clara . . . Get Well
Issued: 1997 • Current
Original Price: $4.00
Value **$4**

5 #2611

Daphne With Dove
Issued: 1995 • Current
Original Price: $4.00
Value **$4**

6 #26003

**Edmund And Bailey . . .
Caroling**
Issued: 1996 • Current
Original Price: $4.00
Value **$4**

THE BEARSTONE COLLECTION
– BEARWEAR PINS –

	Price Paid	Value of My Collection
1.		
2.	✓	
3.		
4.		
5.	✓	
6.		
7.		
8.		

PENCIL TOTALS

7 #26004

**Edmund The Santa
Bear . . . Believe**
Issued: 1996 • Current
Original Price: $4.00
Value **$4**

8 #2631

Elgin The Elf Bear
Issued: 1995 • Current
Original Price: $4.00
Value **$4**

1 #2642

Elliot And The Lights
Issued: 1995 • Current
Original Price: $4.00
Value **$4**

2 #2636

**Elliot Bear With
Jingle Bell Wreath**
Issued: 1995 • Current
Original Price: $4.00
Value **$4**

3 #26001

Elliot . . . The Fireman
Issued: 1996 • Current
Original Price: $4.00
Value **$4**

4 #26002

Elliot With Tree
Issued: 1996 • Current
Original Price: $4.00
Value **$4**

5 #2606

Elliot's Wreath
Issued: 1994 • Current
Original Price: $4.00
Value **$4**

6 #2632

Emma The Witchy Bear
Issued: 1995 • Current
Original Price: $4.00
Value **$4**

7 #26005

**Ernest On The
Pumpkin Wreath**
Issued: 1996 • Current
Original Price: $4.00
Value **$4**

8 #2618

Homer
Issued: 1995 • Out of Production
Original Price: $4.00
Value **$4**

THE BEARSTONE COLLECTION — BEARWEAR PINS —

	Price Paid	Value of My Collection
1.		
2.	✓	
3.		
4.		
5.		
6.		
7.		
8.		

🐾 ✎ **PENCIL TOTALS**

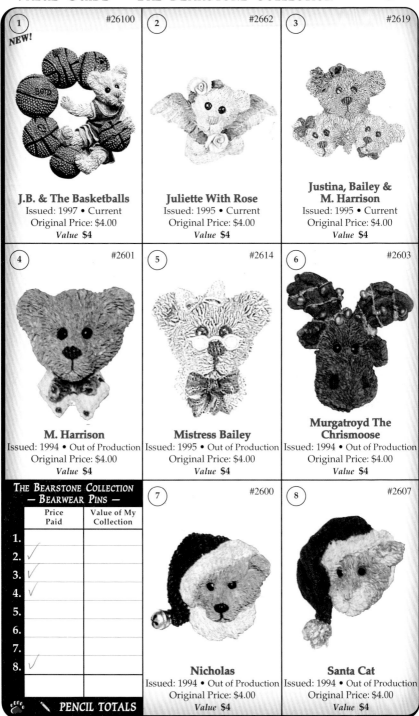

1 NEW! #26100

J.B. & The Basketballs
Issued: 1997 • Current
Original Price: $4.00
Value $4

2 #2662

Juliette With Rose
Issued: 1995 • Current
Original Price: $4.00
Value $4

3 #2619

Justina, Bailey & M. Harrison
Issued: 1995 • Current
Original Price: $4.00
Value $4

4 #2601

M. Harrison
Issued: 1994 • Out of Production
Original Price: $4.00
Value $4

5 #2614

Mistress Bailey
Issued: 1995 • Out of Production
Original Price: $4.00
Value $4

6 #2603

Murgatroyd The Chrismoose
Issued: 1994 • Out of Production
Original Price: $4.00
Value $4

THE BEARSTONE COLLECTION — BEARWEAR PINS —

	Price Paid	Value of My Collection
1.		
2.	✓	
3.	✓	
4.	✓	
5.		
6.		
7.		
8.	✓	

PENCIL TOTALS

7 #2600

Nicholas
Issued: 1994 • Out of Production
Original Price: $4.00
Value $4

8 #2607

Santa Cat
Issued: 1994 • Out of Production
Original Price: $4.00
Value $4

1   #2639

Shelley's Flight
Issued: 1995 • Current
Original Price: $4.00
Value **$4**

2   #2679

Simone In Heart Wreath
Issued: 1995 • Current
Original Price: $4.00
Value **$4**

3   #2610

Springtime Bessie
Issued: 1995 • Out of Production
Original Price: $4.00
Value **$4**

4   NEW!   #26101

Wilson . . . In Love
Issued: 1997 • Current
Original Price: $4.00
Value **$4**

5   #2609

Wilson's Flight
Issued: 1994 • Out of Production
Original Price: $4.00
Value **$4**

THE BEARSTONE COLLECTION
– BEARWEAR PINS –

	Price Paid	Value of My Collection
1.		
2.		
3.		
4.		
5.	✓	
	PENCIL TOTALS	

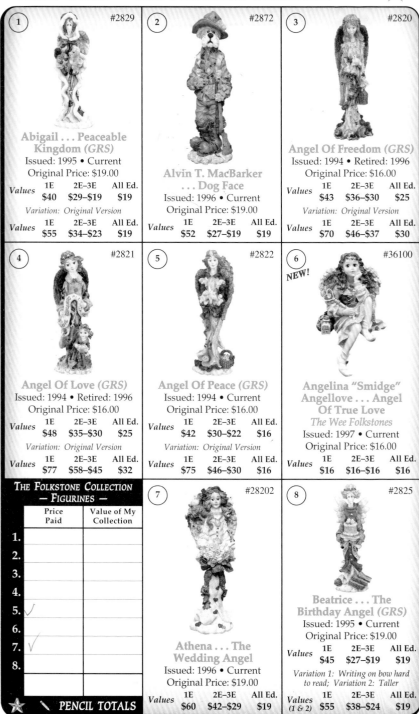

1 #2829

Abigail . . . Peaceable Kingdom *(GRS)*
Issued: 1995 • Current
Original Price: $19.00

Values	1E	2E–3E	All Ed.
	$40	$29–$19	$19

Variation: Original Version

Values	1E	2E–3E	All Ed.
	$55	$34–$23	$19

2 #2872

Alvin T. MacBarker . . . Dog Face
Issued: 1996 • Current
Original Price: $19.00

Values	1E	2E–3E	All Ed.
	$52	$27–$19	$19

3 #2820

Angel Of Freedom *(GRS)*
Issued: 1994 • Retired: 1996
Original Price: $16.00

Values	1E	2E–3E	All Ed.
	$43	$36–$30	$25

Variation: Original Version

Values	1E	2E–3E	All Ed.
	$70	$46–$37	$30

4 #2821

Angel Of Love *(GRS)*
Issued: 1994 • Retired: 1996
Original Price: $16.00

Values	1E	2E–3E	All Ed.
	$48	$35–$30	$25

Variation: Original Version

Values	1E	2E–3E	All Ed.
	$77	$58–$45	$32

5 #2822

Angel Of Peace *(GRS)*
Issued: 1994 • Current
Original Price: $16.00

Values	1E	2E–3E	All Ed.
	$42	$30–$22	$16

Variation: Original Version

Values	1E	2E–3E	All Ed.
	$75	$46–$30	$16

6 NEW! #36100

Angelina "Smidge" Angellove . . . Angel Of True Love
The Wee Folkstones
Issued: 1997 • Current
Original Price: $16.00

Values	1E	2E–3E	All Ed.
	$16	$16–$16	$16

THE FOLKSTONE COLLECTION – FIGURINES –

	Price Paid	Value of My Collection
1.		
2.		
3.		
4.		
5.	✓	
6.		
7.	✓	
8.		

★ ＼ PENCIL TOTALS

7 #28202

Athena . . . The Wedding Angel
Issued: 1996 • Current
Original Price: $19.00

Values	1E	2E–3E	All Ed.
	$60	$42–$29	$19

8 #2825

Beatrice . . . The Birthday Angel *(GRS)*
Issued: 1995 • Current
Original Price: $19.00

Values	1E	2E–3E	All Ed.
	$45	$27–$19	$19

Variation 1: Writing on bow hard to read; Variation 2: Taller

Values (1 & 2)	1E	2E–3E	All Ed.
	$55	$38–$24	$19

1   #2836

Beatrice . . . The Giftgiver
Issued: 1995 • Current
Original Price: $18.00

Values	1E	2E–3E	All Ed.
	$43	$24–$18	$18

2   #2873

Bernie . . . Igotwatiwanted St. Bernard Santa
Issued: 1996 • Current
Original Price: $18.00

Values	1E	2E–3E	All Ed.
	$39	$20–$18	$18

3   #2870

Betty Biscuit
Issued: 1996 • Current
Original Price: $19.00

Values	1E	2E–3E	All Ed.
	N/A	N/A	$19

Variation: "Betty Cocker"

Values	1E	2E–3E	All Ed.
	$80	$56–$40	$19

4   #2831

Boowinkle Von Hindenmoose *(GRS)*
Issued: 1995 • Current
Original Price: $18.00

Values	1E	2E–3E	All Ed.
	$32	$25–$18	$18

Variation: Original Version

Values	1E	2E–3E	All Ed.
	$45	$36–$28	$18

5   #2844

Buster Goes a' Courtin'
Issued: 1996 • Current
Original Price: $19.00

Values	1E	2E–3E	All Ed.
	$50	$33–$19	$19

6   #2811

Chilly & Son With Dove
Issued: 1994 • Current
Original Price: $16.00

Values	1E	2E–3E	All Ed.
	$72	$45–$34	$17

7   #28205

NEW!

Constance & Felicity . . . Best Friend Angels (LE-1997)
Issued: 1997 • Current
Original Price: $38.00

Values	1E	2E–3E	All Ed.
	$38	$38–$38	$38

8   #28201

Cosmos . . . The Gardening Angel
Issued: 1996 • Current
Original Price: $19.00

Values	1E	2E–3E	All Ed.
	$55	$38–$30	$19

The Folkstone Collection – Figurines –

	Price Paid	Value of My Collection
1.		
2.		
3.		
4.		
5.		
6.		
7.		
8.		

✎ PENCIL TOTALS

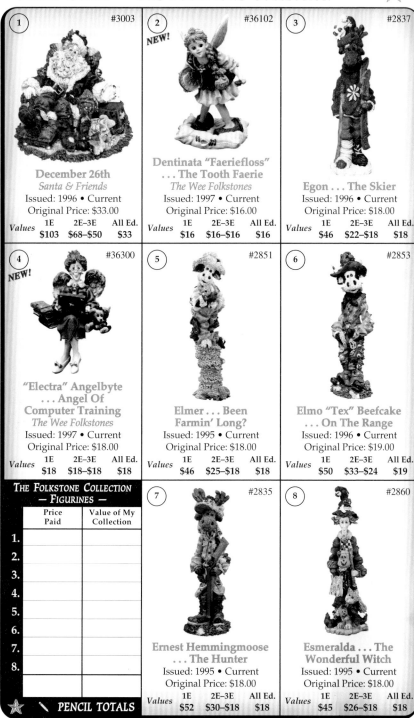

1 #3003

December 26th
Santa & Friends
Issued: 1996 • Current
Original Price: $33.00

Values	1E	2E–3E	All Ed.
	$103	$68–$50	$33

2 NEW! #36102

Dentinata "Faeriefloss" . . . The Tooth Faerie
The Wee Folkstones
Issued: 1997 • Current
Original Price: $16.00

Values	1E	2E–3E	All Ed.
	$16	$16–$16	$16

3 #2837

Egon . . . The Skier
Issued: 1996 • Current
Original Price: $18.00

Values	1E	2E–3E	All Ed.
	$46	$22–$18	$18

4 NEW! #36300

"Electra" Angelbyte . . . Angel Of Computer Training
The Wee Folkstones
Issued: 1997 • Current
Original Price: $18.00

Values	1E	2E–3E	All Ed.
	$18	$18–$18	$18

5 #2851

Elmer . . . Been Farmin' Long?
Issued: 1995 • Current
Original Price: $18.00

Values	1E	2E–3E	All Ed.
	$46	$25–$18	$18

6 #2853

Elmo "Tex" Beefcake . . . On The Range
Issued: 1996 • Current
Original Price: $19.00

Values	1E	2E–3E	All Ed.
	$50	$33–$24	$19

THE FOLKSTONE COLLECTION – FIGURINES –

	Price Paid	Value of My Collection
1.		
2.		
3.		
4.		
5.		
6.		
7.		
8.		

PENCIL TOTALS

7 #2835

Ernest Hemmingmoose . . . The Hunter
Issued: 1995 • Current
Original Price: $18.00

Values	1E	2E–3E	All Ed.
	$52	$30–$18	$18

8 #2860

Esmeralda . . . The Wonderful Witch
Issued: 1995 • Current
Original Price: $18.00

Values	1E	2E–3E	All Ed.
	$45	$26–$18	$18

THE FOLKSTONE COLLECTION

1 #36301

NEW!

Estudious "Cram" Faeriebaum ... The Study Faerie
The Wee Folkstones
Issued: 1997 • Current
Original Price: $18.00

Values	1E	2E–3E	All Ed.
	$18	$18–$18	$18

2 #28203-06

Etheral ... Angel Of Light (LE-7,200)
Issued: 1996 • Retired: 1996
Original Price: $19.00
Value $165

3 #3600

Fixit ... Santa's Faerie
The Wee Folkstones
Issued: 1996 • Current
Original Price: $18.00

Values	1E	2E–3E	All Ed.
	$50	$38–$25	$18

4 #2846

Flora, Amelia & Eloise ... The Tea Party
Issued: 1996 • Current
Original Price: $19.00

Values	1E	2E–3E	All Ed.
	$50	$30–$19	$19

5 #2843

Flora & Amelia ... The Gardeners
Issued: 1996 • Current
Original Price: $19.00

Values	1E	2E–3E	All Ed.
	$55	$35–$19	$19

6 #2824

Florence ... The Kitchen Angel (GRS)
Issued: 1995 • Retired: 1996
Original Price: $19.00

Values	1E	2E–3E	All Ed.
	$48	$40–$32	$28

Variation 1: Hand on bottom center of bowl; Variation 2: Longer skirt

Values (1 & 2)	1E	2E–3E	All Ed.
	$55	$42–$37	$32

7 #2833

Ichabod Mooselman ... The Pilgrim
Issued: 1995 • Current
Original Price: $18.00

Values	1E	2E–3E	All Ed.
	$44	$20–$18	$18

8 #2852

Ida & Bessie ... The Gardeners (GRS)
Issued: 1995 • Current
Original Price: $18.00

Values	1E	2E–3E	All Ed.
	$38	$20–$18	$18

Variation: Original Version

Values	1E	2E–3E	All Ed.
	$50	$33–$25	$18

THE FOLKSTONE COLLECTION – FIGURINES –

	Price Paid	Value of My Collection
1.		
2.		
3.		
4.		
5.		
6.		
7.		
8.		

✏ PENCIL TOTALS

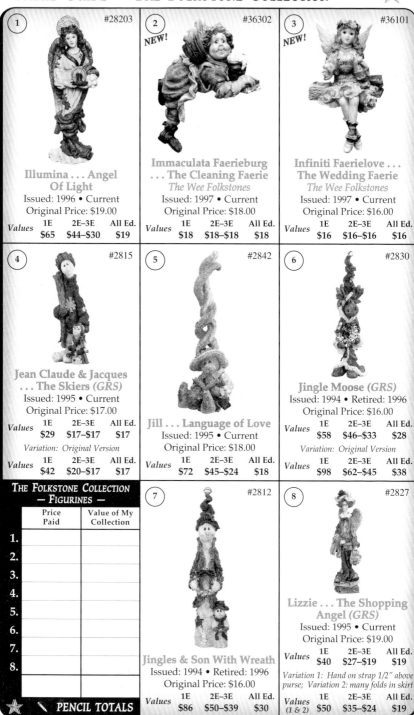

1   #28203

Illumina . . . Angel Of Light
Issued: 1996 • Current
Original Price: $19.00

Values	1E	2E–3E	All Ed.
	$65	$44–$30	$19

2   NEW!   #36302

Immaculata Faerieburg . . . The Cleaning Faerie
The Wee Folkstones
Issued: 1997 • Current
Original Price: $18.00

Values	1E	2E–3E	All Ed.
	$18	$18–$18	$18

3   NEW!   #36101

Infiniti Faerielove . . . The Wedding Faerie
The Wee Folkstones
Issued: 1997 • Current
Original Price: $16.00

Values	1E	2E–3E	All Ed.
	$16	$16–$16	$16

4   #2815

Jean Claude & Jacques . . . The Skiers *(GRS)*
Issued: 1995 • Current
Original Price: $17.00

Values	1E	2E–3E	All Ed.
	$29	$17–$17	$17

Variation: Original Version

Values	1E	2E–3E	All Ed.
	$42	$20–$17	$17

5   #2842

Jill . . . Language of Love
Issued: 1995 • Current
Original Price: $18.00

Values	1E	2E–3E	All Ed.
	$72	$45–$24	$18

6   #2830

Jingle Moose *(GRS)*
Issued: 1994 • Retired: 1996
Original Price: $16.00

Values	1E	2E–3E	All Ed.
	$58	$46–$33	$28

Variation: Original Version

Values	1E	2E–3E	All Ed.
	$98	$62–$45	$38

THE FOLKSTONE COLLECTION – FIGURINES –

	Price Paid	Value of My Collection
1.		
2.		
3.		
4.		
5.		
6.		
7.		
8.		

PENCIL TOTALS

7   #2812

Jingles & Son With Wreath
Issued: 1994 • Retired: 1996
Original Price: $16.00

Values	1E	2E–3E	All Ed.
	$86	$50–$39	$30

8   #2827

Lizzie . . . The Shopping Angel *(GRS)*
Issued: 1995 • Current
Original Price: $19.00

Values	1E	2E–3E	All Ed.
	$40	$27–$19	$19

Variation 1: Hand on strap 1/2" above purse; Variation 2: many folds in skirt

Values (1 & 2)	1E	2E–3E	All Ed.
	$50	$35–$24	$19

1   #2854

**Loretta Moostein...
"Yer Cheatin' Heart"**
Issued: 1996 • Current
Original Price: $19.00

Values	1E	2E–3E	All Ed.
	$42	$22–$19	$19

2   NEW!   #28240

Mercy... Angel Of Nurses
Issued: 1997 • Current
Original Price: $19.00

Values	1E	2E–3E	All Ed.
	$19	$19–$19	$19

3   #2826

**Minerva... The
Baseball Angel**
Issued: 1995 • Current
Original Price: $19.00

Values	1E	2E–3E	All Ed.
	$50	$25–$19	$19

Variation: 6 buttons below belt

Values	1E	2E–3E	All Ed.
	$50	$25–$19	$19

4   NEW!   #28241

**Ms. Patience... Angel
Of Teachers**
Issued: 1997 • Current
Original Price: $19.00

Values	1E	2E–3E	All Ed.
	$19	$19–$19	$19

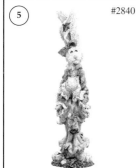

5   #2840

Myrtle... Believe!
Issued: 1995 • Current
Original Price: $18.00

Values	1E	2E–3E	All Ed.
	$52	$28–$18	$18

6   #2807

**Na-Nick And Siegfried
... The Plan (LE-10,000)**
Issued: 1996 • Retired: 1996
Original Price: $34.00
Value **$130**

7   #2804

Na-Nick Of The North (GRS)
Issued: 1995 • Current
Original Price: $18.00

Values	1E	2E–3E	All Ed.
	$48	$29–$18	$18

Variation: Original Version

Values	1E	2E–3E	All Ed.
	$58	$37–$24	$18

8   #2817

Nanny... The Snowmom
Issued: 1996 • Current
Original Price: $18.00

Values	1E	2E–3E	All Ed.
	$47	$26–$18	$18

**THE FOLKSTONE COLLECTION
— FIGURINES —**

	Price Paid	Value of My Collection
1.		
2.		
3.		
4.		
5.		
6.		
7.		
8.		

\ PENCIL TOTALS

THE FOLKSTONE COLLECTION

1 #2800

Nicholai With Tree
Issued: 1994 • Current
Original Price: $17.00

Values	1E	2E–3E	All Ed.
	$81	$40–$27	$17

2 #2802

Nicholas With Book Of Lists
Issued: 1994 • Retired: 1996
Original Price: $17.00

Values	1E	2E–3E	All Ed.
	$80	$42–$33	$27

3 #3001

Nick On Ice (GRS)
Santa & Friends
Issued: 1994 • Current
Original Price: $33.00

Values	1E	2E–3E	All Ed.
	$75	$48–$39	$33

Variation: Original Version

Values	1E	2E–3E	All Ed.
	$108	$69–$55	$33

4 #2806

Nicknoah . . . Santa With Ark
Issued: 1996 • Current
Original Price: $18.00

Values	1E	2E–3E	All Ed.
	$50	$32–$23	$18

5 #2801

Niki With Candle
Issued: 1994 • Current
Original Price: $17.00

Values	1E	2E–3E	All Ed.
	$73	$36–$28	$17

6 #2805

No-No-Nick . . . Bad Boy Santa
Issued: 1996 • Current
Original Price: $18.00

Values	1E	2E–3E	All Ed.
	$50	$32–$23	$18

THE FOLKSTONE COLLECTION – FIGURINES –

	Price Paid	Value of My Collection
1.		
2.		
3.		
4.		
5. √		
6.		
7.		
8.		

PENCIL TOTALS

7 #2814

Northbound Willie (GRS)
Issued: 1995 • Current
Original Price: $17.00

Values	1E	2E–3E	All Ed.
	$36	$24–$17	$17

Variation: Original Version

Values	1E	2E–3E	All Ed.
	$53	$35–$24	$17

8 #2823

Oceania . . . Ocean Angel (GRS)
Issued: 1995 • Current
Original Price: $16.00

Values	1E	2E–3E	All Ed.
	$50	$32–$23	$16

Variation: Original Version

Values	1E	2E–3E	All Ed.
	$88	$50–$32	$16

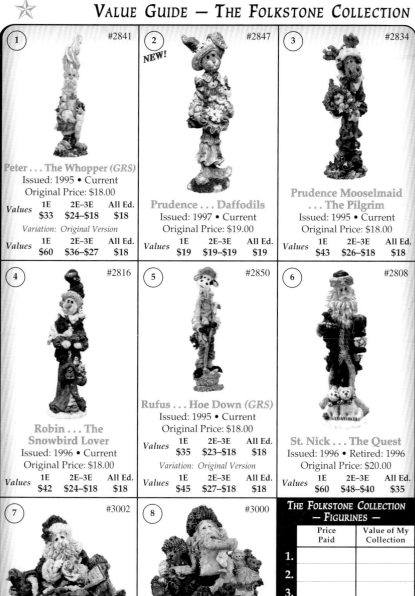

1 #2841

Peter . . . The Whopper *(GRS)*
Issued: 1995 • Current
Original Price: $18.00

Values	1E	2E–3E	All Ed.
	$33	$24–$18	$18

Variation: Original Version

Values	1E	2E–3E	All Ed.
	$60	$36–$27	$18

2 NEW! #2847

Prudence . . . Daffodils
Issued: 1997 • Current
Original Price: $19.00

Values	1E	2E–3E	All Ed.
	$19	$19–$19	$19

3 #2834

**Prudence Mooselmaid
. . . The Pilgrim**
Issued: 1995 • Current
Original Price: $18.00

Values	1E	2E–3E	All Ed.
	$43	$26–$18	$18

4 #2816

**Robin . . . The
Snowbird Lover**
Issued: 1996 • Current
Original Price: $18.00

Values	1E	2E–3E	All Ed.
	$42	$24–$18	$18

5 #2850

Rufus . . . Hoe Down *(GRS)*
Issued: 1995 • Current
Original Price: $18.00

Values	1E	2E–3E	All Ed.
	$35	$23–$18	$18

Variation: Original Version

Values	1E	2E–3E	All Ed.
	$45	$27–$18	$18

6 #2808

St. Nick . . . The Quest
Issued: 1996 • Retired: 1996
Original Price: $20.00

Values	1E	2E–3E	All Ed.
	$60	$48–$40	$35

7 #3002

Santa's Challenge *(GRS)*
Santa & Friends
Issued: 1994 • Current
Original Price: $33.00

Values	1E	2E–3E	All Ed.
	$70	$55–$44	$33

Variation: Original Version

Values	1E	2E–3E	All Ed.
	$100	$68–$55	$33

8 #3000

Santa's Flight Plan *(GRS)*
Santa & Friends
Issued: 1994 • Current
Original Price: $33.00

Values	1E	2E–3E	All Ed.
	$65	$55–$45	$33

Variation: Original Version

Values	1E	2E–3E	All Ed.
	$102	$68–$55	$33

THE FOLKSTONE COLLECTION
– FIGURINES –

	Price Paid	Value of My Collection
1.		
2.		
3.		
4.		
5.		
6.		
7.		
8.		

PENCIL TOTALS

① #3004

Santa's Hobby . . . The Teddy Bear Maker
Santa & Friends
Issued: 1996 • Current
Original Price: $35.00

Values	1E	2E–3E	All Ed.
	$68	$55–$48	$35

② #2828

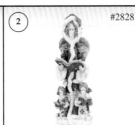

Seraphina With Jacob & Rachael . . . The Choir Angels
Issued: 1995 • Current
Original Price: $20.00

Values	1E	2E–3E	All Ed.
	$35	$26–$20	$20

Variation: Original Version

Values	1E	2E–3E	All Ed.
	$47	$31–$20	$20

③ #28204

Serenity . . . The Mother's Angel
Issued: 1996 • Current
Original Price: $19.00

Values	1E	2E–3E	All Ed.
	$48	$30–$19	$19

④ #2874
NEW!

Sgt. Rex & Matt . . . The Runaway
Issued: 1997 • Current
Original Price: $19.50

Values	1E	2E–3E	All Ed.
	$19.50	$19.50	$19.50

⑤ #2899

Siegfried & Egon . . . The Sign (GRS)
Issued: 1995 • Current
Original Price: $17.00

Values	1E	2E–3E	All Ed.
	$33	$24–$17	$17

Variation: Original Version

Values	1E	2E–3E	All Ed.
	$55	$34–$22	$17

⑥ #2803

Sliknick . . . The Chimney Sweep (GRS)
Issued: 1995 • Current
Original Price: $18.00

Values	1E	2E–3E	All Ed.
	$40	$27–$18	$18

Variation: Original Version

Values	1E	2E–3E	All Ed.
	$52	$34–$22	$18

THE FOLKSTONE COLLECTION — FIGURINES —

	Price Paid	Value of My Collection
1.		
2.		
3.		
4.		
5.		
6.		
7.		
8.		

⭐ PENCIL TOTALS

⑦ #2871

Sparky McPlug
Issued: 1996 • Current
Original Price: $19.00

Values	1E	2E–3E	All Ed.
	$45	$26–$19	$19

⑧ #2845

"Too Loose" Lapin . . . "The Arte-e-st"
Issued: 1996 • Current
Original Price: $19.00

Values	1E	2E–3E	All Ed.
	$45	$25–$19	$19

1 #2810

Windy With Book
Issued: 1994 • Retired: 1996
Original Price: $16.00

Values	1E	2E–3E	All Ed.
	$84	$58–$43	$32

2 NEW! #2838

Ziggy ... The Duffer
Issued: 1997 • Current
Original Price: $19.00

Values	1E	2E–3E	All Ed.
	$19	$19–$19	$19

3 NEW! #BC361021

Dentinata Canadian Tooth Faerie
Issued: 1997 • Current
Original Price: $24.99 (Canadian)

Values (U.S.)	1E	2E–3E	All Ed.
	$30	$30–$30	$30

4 #2564

Chilly With Wreath
Issued: 1996 • Current
Original Price: $10.00
Value **$10**

5 #2553

Father Christmas
Issued: 1995 • Current
Original Price: $10.00
Value **$10**

6 #2561

Jean Claude & Jacque ... The Skiers
Issued: 1995 • Current
Original Price: $10.00
Value **$10**

7 #2562

Jingles The Snowman With Wreath
Issued: 1995 • Current
Original Price: $10.00
Value **$10**

THE FOLKSTONE COLLECTION
— FIGURINES —

	Price Paid	Value of My Collection
1.		
2.		

— CANADIAN FIGURINES —

3.		

— ORNAMENTS —

4.		
5.		
6.		
7.		

⭐ ＼ PENCIL TOTALS

61

#2550

Nicholai With Tree
Issued: 1995 • Current
Original Price: $10.00
Value **$10**

#2551

Nicholas The Giftgiver
Issued: 1995 • Current
Original Price: $10.00
Value **$10**

#2560

Olaf . . . Let It Snow
Issued: 1995 • Current
Original Price: $10.00
Value **$10**

#2552

Sliknick In The Chimney
Issued: 1995 • Current
Original Price: $10.00
Value **$10**

#2565

Willie With Broom
Issued: 1996 • Current
Original Price: $10.00
Value **$10**

#2563

Windy With Tree
Issued: 1996 • Current
Original Price: $10.00
Value **$10**

THE FOLKSTONE COLLECTION
— ORNAMENTS —

	Price Paid	Value of My Collection
1.		
2.		
3.		
4.		
5.		
6.		

— WATERGLOBES —

7.		
8.		

PENCIL TOTALS

#2710

Jean Claude & Jacques . . . The Skiers
Issued: 1996 • Current
Original Price: $37.00

Values	1E	2E–3E	All Ed.
	$37	$37–$37	$37

#2703

Santa's Flight Plan
Issued: 1995 • Retired: 1996
Original Price: $36.00
Value **$65**

1   #2666

Alice & Emily
Issued: 1996 • Current
Original Price: $4.00
Value **$4**

2   #2671

Ariel . . . The Guardian
Issued: 1996 • Current
Original Price: $4.00
Value **$4**

3   #26303

Ashley The Angel
Issued: 1996 • Current
Original Price: $4.00
Value **$4**

4 NEW!   #26404

Baby Amelia's Carrot Juice
Issued: 1997 • Current
Original Price: $4.00
Value **$4**

5   #2638

Beatrice's Wreath
Issued: 1995 • Current
Original Price: $4.00
Value **$4**

6   #2664

Bessie With Sun Flowers
Issued: 1996 • Current
Original Price: $4.00
Value **$4**

7 NEW!   #26403

Betty Biscuit
Issued: 1997 • Current`
Original Price: $4.00
Value **$4**

8   #2668

Daphne In Straw Hat
Issued: 1996 • Current
Original Price: $4.00
Value **$4**

THE FOLKSTONE COLLECTION

	Price Paid	Value of My Collection
1.		
2.		
3.		
4.		
5.		
6.		
7.		
8.		
★	\ **PENCIL TOTALS**	

THE FOLKSTONE COLLECTION
— FOLKWEAR PINS —

THE FOLKSTONE COLLECTION

1 #2661

Eloise In The Cabbage Patch
Issued: 1996 • Current
Original Price: $4.00
Value **$4**

2 #26402

NEW!

Eloise . . . Tea Toter
Issued: 1997 • Current
Original Price: $4.00
Value **$4**

3 #26304

Esmeralda The Witch
Issued: 1996 • Current
Original Price: $4.00
Value **$4**

4 #2625

Florence Wings It
Issued: 1995 • Current
Original Price: $4.00
Value **$4**

5 #26400

NEW!

Florina's Wreath
Issued: 1997 • Current
Original Price: $4.00
Value **$4**

6 #2651

Jean Claude The Skier
Issued: 1995 • Current
Original Price: $4.00
Value **$4**

The Folkstone Collection
— Folkwear Pins —

	Price Paid	Value of My Collection
1.		
2.		
3.		
4.		
5.		
6.		
7.		
8.		

PENCIL TOTALS

7 #26302

Jingles With Wreath
Issued: 1996 • Current
Original Price: $4.00
Value **$4**

8 #2658

Minerva With Daffodils
Issued: 1996 • Current
Original Price: $4.00
Value **$4**

1   #2647

Minerva's Flight
Issued: 1995 • Current
Original Price: $4.00
Value $4

2   #26401

NEW!

**Ms. Patience . . .
The Teacher**
Issued: 1997 • Current
Original Price: $4.00
Value $4

3   #2650

Na-Nick Of The North
Issued: 1995 • Current
Original Price: $4.00
Value $4

4   #26300

Nicholai With Tree
Issued: 1996 • Current
Original Price: $4.00
Value $4

5   #2648

Nicholia . . . With Dove
Issued: 1995 • Current
Original Price: $4.00
Value $4

6   #2649

Nicholas . . . With Tree
Issued: 1995 • Current
Original Price: $4.00
Value $4

7   #2674

Oceania
Issued: 1996 • Current
Original Price: $4.00
Value $4

8   #2669

Ralph Angel Pooch
Issued: 1996 • Current
Original Price: $4.00
Value $4

THE FOLKSTONE COLLECTION — FOLKWEAR PINS —

	Price Paid	Value of My Collection
1.		
2.		
3.		
4.		
5.		
6.		
7.		
8.	✓	

✦   ＼ **PENCIL TOTALS** ╱

THE FOLKSTONE COLLECTION

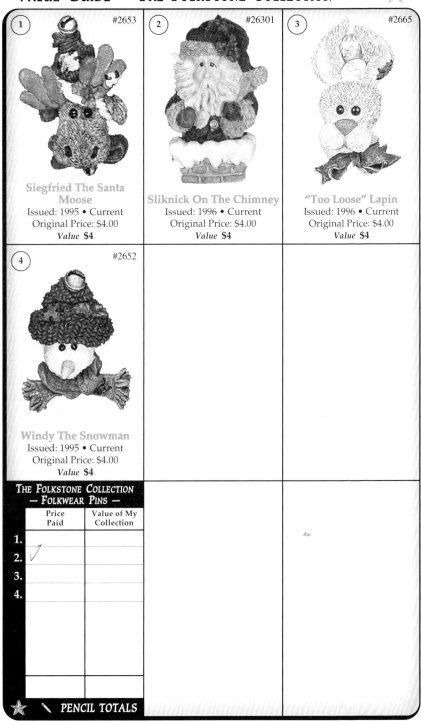

1   #2653

Siegfried The Santa Moose
Issued: 1995 • Current
Original Price: $4.00
Value **$4**

2   #26301

Sliknick On The Chimney
Issued: 1996 • Current
Original Price: $4.00
Value **$4**

3   #2665

"Too Loose" Lapin
Issued: 1996 • Current
Original Price: $4.00
Value **$4**

4   #2652

Windy The Snowman
Issued: 1995 • Current
Original Price: $4.00
Value **$4**

THE FOLKSTONE COLLECTION — FOLKWEAR PINS —

	Price Paid	Value of My Collection
1.		
2.	✓	
3.		
4.		

⭐   **\ PENCIL TOTALS**

1 #3518

NEW!

**The Amazing Bailey . . .
"Magic Show At 4" (LE-1997)**
Issued: 1997 • Current
Original Price: $58.00
Value **$58**
Variation: Premier Edition
Original Price: $56.00
Value **$56**

2 #3599

Anne . . . The Masterpiece
Issued: 1996 • Current
Original Price: $25.00

Values	1E	2E–3E	All Ed.
	$65	$35–$25	$25

3 #3506

**Ashley With Chrissie
. . . Dress Up**
Issued: 1996 • Current
Original Price: $20.50

Values	1E	2E–3E	All Ed.
	$60	$32–$24	$20.50

Variation: Premier Edition
Original Price: $22.00
Value **$68**

4 #3503

**Betsey With Edmund . . .
The Patriots**
Issued: 1996 • Current
Original Price: $20.00

Values	1E	2E–3E	All Ed.
	$74	$43–$32	$20

Variation: Premier Edition
Original Price: $19.50
Value **$128**

5 #3514

**Candice With Matthew
. . . Gathering Apples**
Issued: 1996 • Current
Original Price: $19.00

Values	1E	2E–3E	All Ed.
	$52	$29–$23	$19

Variation: Premier Edition
Original Price: $21.00
Value **$61**

6 #3512

**Courtney With Phoebe
. . . Over The River And
Thru The Woods**
Issued: 1996 • Current
Original Price: $25.00

Values	1E	2E–3E	All Ed.
	$60	$30–$25	$25

7 #3512-01

**Courtney With Phoebe
. . . Over The River And
Thru The Woods
(GCC Exclusive)**
Issued: 1996 • Retired: 1996
Original Price: $27.50

Values	1E	2E–3E	All Ed.
	$80	$49–$41	$35

8 #3508

**Emily With Kathleen &
Otis . . . The Future**
Issued: 1996 • Current
Original Price: $30.00

Values	1E	2E–3E	All Ed.
	$72	$45–$35	$30

Variation: Premier Edition
Original Price: $27.00
Value **$93**

THE DOLLSTONE COLLECTION — FIGURINES

	Price Paid	Value of My Collection
1.		
2.		
3.		
4.		
5.		
6.		
7.		
8.		

＼ PENCIL TOTALS

THE DOLLSTONE COLLECTION

1 #3510

Jean With Elliot & Debbie ... The Bakers
Issued: 1996 • Current
Original Price: $20.00

Values	1E	2E–3E	All Ed.
	$52	$30–$20	$20

Variation: Premier Edition
Original Price: $22.00
Value $64

Variation: Kirlin's exclusive
Value N/E (not established)

---

2 #3500

Jennifer With Priscilla ... The Doll In The Attic
Issued: 1996 • Current
Original Price: $20.50

Values	1E	2E–3E	All Ed.
	$85	$49–$36	$20.50

Variation: Premier Edition (sold in stores)
Original Price: $20.50
Value $165

---

3 NEW! #3520

Julia With Emmy Lou & Daphne ... Garden Friends
Issued: 1997 • Current
Original Price: $20.00

Values	1E	2E–3E	All Ed.
	$20	$20–$20	$20

Variation: Premier Edition
Original Price: $20.00
Value $20

---

4 #3515

Karen With Wilson & Eloise ... Mother's Present
Issued: 1996 • Current
Original Price: $26.00

Values	1E	2E–3E	All Ed.
	$65	$48–$41	$32

---

5 #3505

Katherine With Edmund & Amanda ... Kind Hearts
Issued: 1996 • Current
Original Price: $20.00

Values	1E	2E–3E	All Ed.
	$79	$49–$39	$20

Variation: Premier Edition
Original Price: $19.50
Value $145

---

6 #3516

Kristi With Nicole ... Skater's Waltz (GCC Exclusive)
Issued: 1996 • Retired: 1996
Original Price: $26.00

Values	1E	2E–3E	All Ed.
	$70	$54–$45	$32

THE DOLLSTONE COLLECTION — FIGURINES —

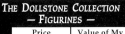

	Price Paid	Value of My Collection
1.		
2.		
3.		
4.		
5.		
6.		
7.		
8.		

✎ **PENCIL TOTALS**

---

7 NEW! #3522

Laura With Jane ... First Day Of School
Issued: 1997 • Current
Original Price: $23.00

Values	1E	2E–3E	All Ed.
	$23	$23–$23	$23

Variation: Premier Edition
Original Price: $23.00
Value $23

---

8 #3517V

Mallory With Patsy & J.B. Bean ... Trick Or Treat (Premier Edition only)
Issued: 1996 • Current
Original Price: $27.00
Value $130

1 #3504

Megan With Elliot & Annie ... Christmas Carol
Issued: 1996 • Current
Original Price: $20.00

Values	1E	2E–3E	All Ed.
	$65	$40–$30	$20

Variation: Premier Edition
Original Price: $20.00
Value $325

2 #3511

Michelle With Daisy ... Reading Is Fun
Issued: 1996 • Current
Original Price: $18.00

Values	1E	2E–3E	All Ed.
	$42	$25–$18	$18

Variation: Premier Edition
Original Price: $20.00
Value $68

3 #3519

NEW!

Natalie With Joy ... Sunday School
Issued: 1997 • Current
Original Price: $23.00

Values	1E	2E–3E	All Ed.
	$23	$23–$23	$23

4 #3501

Patricia With Molly ... Attic Treasures
Issued: 1996 • Current
Original Price: $14.00

Values	1E	2E–3E	All Ed.
	$72	$44–$36	$14

Variation: Premier Edition (sold in stores)
Original Price: $14.00
Value $150

5 #3509

Rebecca With Elliot ... Birthday
Issued: 1996 • Current
Original Price: $20.50

Values	1E	2E–3E	All Ed.
	$60	$38–$30	$20.50

Variation: Premier Edition
Original Price: $22.00
Value $73

6 #3507

Sarah & Heather With Elliot, Dolly & Amelia ... Tea For Four (LE-1996)
Issued: 1996 • Retired: 1996
Original Price: $47.00

Values	1E	2E–3E	All Ed.
	$112	$85–$73	$62

Variation: Premier Edition
Original Price: $42.00
Value $155

7 #3502

Victoria With Samantha ... Victorian Ladies
Issued: 1996 • Current
Original Price: $20.00

Values	1E	2E–3E	All Ed.
	$70	$52–$45	$20

Variation: Premier Edition
Original Price: $19.95
Value $143

8 #3521

NEW!

Wendy With Bronte, Keats, Tennyson & Poe ... Wash Day
Issued: 1997 • Current
Original Price: $23.00

Values	1E	2E–3E	All Ed.
	$23	$23–$23	$23

Variation: Premier Edition
Original Price: $23.00
Value $23

THE DOLLSTONE COLLECTION – FIGURINES –

	Price Paid	Value of My Collection
1.		
2.		
3.		
4.		
5.		
6.		
7.		
8.		

PENCIL TOTALS

THE DOLLSTONE COLLECTION

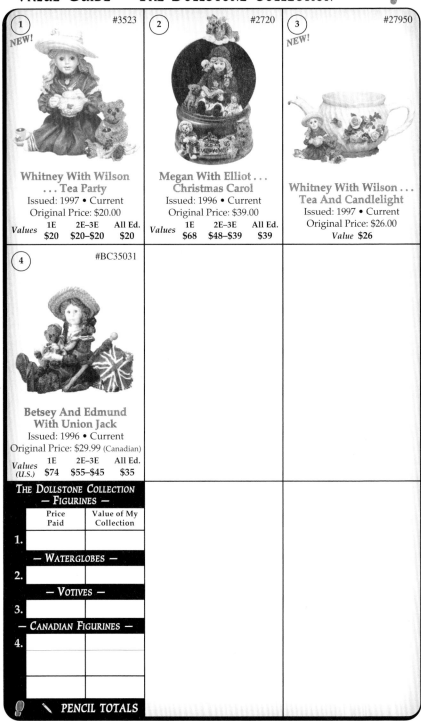

1 #3523

NEW!

Whitney With Wilson ... Tea Party
Issued: 1997 • Current
Original Price: $20.00

Values	1E	2E–3E	All Ed.
	$20	$20–$20	$20

2 #2720

Megan With Elliot ... Christmas Carol
Issued: 1996 • Current
Original Price: $39.00

Values	1E	2E–3E	All Ed.
	$68	$48–$39	$39

3 #27950

NEW!

Whitney With Wilson ... Tea And Candlelight
Issued: 1997 • Current
Original Price: $26.00
Value **$26**

4 #BC35031

Betsey And Edmund With Union Jack
Issued: 1996 • Current
Original Price: $29.99 (Canadian)

Values (U.S.)	1E	2E–3E	All Ed.
	$74	$55–$45	$35

THE DOLLSTONE COLLECTION
– FIGURINES –

	Price Paid	Value of My Collection
1.		
– WATERGLOBES –		
2.		
– VOTIVES –		
3.		
– CANADIAN FIGURINES –		
4.		

✏ PENCIL TOTALS

1 #3200

Augustus "Gus" Grizberg
Issued: 1996 • Current
Original Price: $19.00

Values	1E	2E–3E	All Ed.
	$19	$19–$19	$19

2 #3201

Gertrude "Gertie" Grizberg
Issued: 1996 • Current
Original Price: $15.00

Values	1E	2E–3E	All Ed.
	$15	$15–$15	$15

3 #3201-01

Gladys
Issued: 1996 • Retired: 1996
Original Price: $15.00

Values	1E	2E–3E	All Ed.
	$15	$15–$15	$15

4 #3203

NEW!

Maisey "The Goil" Grizberg
Issued: 1997 • Current
Original Price: $10.00

Values	1E	2E–3E	All Ed.
	$10	$10–$10	$10

5 #3204-01

NEW!

Santa Shoe Box Bear (NALED Exclusive)
Issued: 1997 • Current
Original Price: N/A

Values	1E	2E–3E	All Ed.
	N/A	N/A	N/A

6 #3202

Thaddeus "Bud" Grizberg
Issued: 1996 • Current
Original Price: $10.00

Values	1E	2E–3E	All Ed.
	$10	$10–$10	$10

THE SHOE BOX BEARS — FIGURINES —

	Price Paid	Value of My Collection
1.		
2.		
3.		
4.		
5.		
6.		

 ✎ PENCIL TOTALS

THE SHOE BOX BEARS

(1) #01996-31

Raeburn (6" plush bear)
Issued: 1996 • Current
Original Price: NFS
Value N/E (not established)

(2) #01996-21

Uncle Elliot (pin)
Issued: 1996 • Current
Original Price: NFS
Value N/E (not established)

(3) #01996-11

Uncle Elliot . . . The Head Bean Wants You (figurine)
Issued: 1996 • Current
Original Price: NFS
Value N/E (not established)

(4) #01996-51
NEW!

Velma Q. Berriweather . . . The Cookie Queen (11" plush bear)
Issued: 1997 • Current
Original Price: $29.00
Value **$29**

(5) #01996-41
NEW!

Velma Q. Berriweather . . . The Cookie Queen (figurine)
Issued: 1997 • Current
Original Price: $19.00
Value **$19**

COLLECTOR'S CLUB — MEMBERSHIP PIECES —		
	Price Paid	Value of My Collection
1.		
2.		
3.		
4.		
5.		
PENCIL TOTALS		

Use these pages to record future Boyds resin releases.

THE BEARSTONE COLLECTION	Orig. Price	Status	Market Value			Price Paid	Value of My Collection
			1E	3E-2E	All Ed.		

THE FOLKSTONE COLLECTION							

PENCIL TOTALS

PRICE PAID	MARKET VALUE

Use these pages to record future Boyds resin releases.

THE DOLLSTONE COLLECTION	Orig. Price	Status	Market Value			Price Paid	Value of My Collection
			1E	3E-2E	All Ed.		
THE SHOE BOX BEARS							
COLLECTOR'S CLUB PIECES							
PENCIL TOTALS						Price Paid	Market Value

Total Value Of My Collection

Record the value of your collection here by adding the pencil totals from the bottom of each value guide page.

THE BEARSTONE COLLECTION	Price Paid	Market Value
Page 29		
Page 30		
Page 31		
Page 32		
Page 33		
Page 34		
Page 35		
Page 36		
Page 37		
Page 38		
Page 39		
Page 40		
Page 41		
Page 42		
Page 43		
Page 44		
Page 45		
Page 46		
Page 47		
Page 48		
Page 49		
Page 50		
Page 51		
Page 73		
TOTAL		

THE FOLKSTONE COLLECTION	Price Paid	Market Value
Page 52		
Page 53		
Page 54		
Page 55		
Page 56		
Page 57		
Page 58		
Page 59		
Page 60		
Page 61		
Page 62		
Page 63		
Page 64		
Page 65		
Page 66		
Page 73		
TOTAL		

THE DOLLSTONE COLLECTION	Price Paid	Market Value
Page 64		
Page 65		
Page 66		
Page 67		
Page 68		
Page 69		
Page 70		
Page 74		
TOTAL		

THE SHOE BOX BEARS/ COLLECTOR'S CLUB PIECES	Price Paid	Market Value
Page 71		
Page 72		
Page 74		
TOTAL		

GRAND TOTALS		
	PRICE PAID	MARKET VALUE

Boyds Plush Overview

With years of experience in both clothing design and retailing in his pocket, Gary Lowenthal (known to many as the "Head Bean") embarked on his first big foray into the animal kingdom in 1987 by introducing a line of plush bears, hares, cats, moose and other creatures under the banner of The Boyds Collection Ltd. The "Head Bean" had no idea the line would be so successful; he had never intended the critters to be collectibles, only to be "slightly off-center" and fun!

There have been over 600 animals in a number of unique series in the award-winning Boyds plush line. The plush animals, many of which are fully-jointed, are offered in a variety of different materials and sizes.  There are stylish bears in soft woolly sweaters and floral dresses, as well as those sly little ones who try to disguise themselves as bunnies and cats and even some mice that adorn hats resembling vegetables. Accessory items from eyeglasses to vests to wicker furniture add even more detail to the collection. And it doesn't stop there! The creative juices at The Boyds Collection Ltd. have been flowing freely with 55 new plush characters and ornaments for the Spring of 1997. The section that follows describes each plush series featuring new releases in alphabetical order.

Animal Menagerie . . . There is quite an assortment of bean bag animals to choose from down on the farm in *Animal Menagerie.* In 1997, four new tenants can be seen hanging around the water troughs: the dignified (as dignified as pigs can be – but who can argue with names like this?) "Sheffield O'Swine" and "Lofton Q. McSwine" and two monkeys, "Finster R. Tsuris" and "Imogene R. Tsuris."

The Archive Series . . . Gary Lowenthal's passion for antiques is the foundation of *The Archive Series,* a line based on the simple style of the classic teddy bear. These poseable animals are fully jointed and hand-

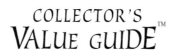

embroidered, offering a bit of tradition and class to the world of plush. In 1997, there is one addition to *The Archive Series,* the off-white chenille bear "Hubbard W. Growler."

Artisan Series . . . Designed in conjunction with various "up-and-coming" artists, this grouping has seen four rabbits and two birds pass through since 1995. Retirements will take their toll, however, and by the end of the year, the only current plush character in this series will be "Roxbunny R. Hare," a new long-eared bunny.

Bears In The Attic . . . Everyone remembers their tattered teddy bears, worn out by years and years of too much love and in the *Bears In The Attic* series, The Boyds Collection Ltd. strives to recapture these memories. Formed from chenille and sherpa pile, these valued companions are as soft and cuddly as those that are well-worn from too many hugs. The latest discovery in the attic is the treasured bear "Tremont."

The Choir Bears . . . If you listen very carefully, you may hear the heavenly tunes of *The Choir Bears* filling the hallways of The Boyds Collection Ltd. These saintly critters are designed to sit on a shelf, lay down and even kneel. In 1997, this exclusive order of bears welcomes hare "Brigham Boneah" into the circle.

Clintons Cabinet . . . It's been a tumultuous year in the cabinet, with an inauguration and three retirements. Fortunately, there are two new faces that will bring fresh political blood to the table this year. However, you probably won't find the stately "Morris" or the virtuous "Artemus" trying to paw their way into the political spotlight!

Grizzly Bears . . . This collection of not-so-ferocious grizzlies make their homes in the wilds of The Boyds Collection Ltd. Out of the thicket, walking arm-in-arm, come the newest members of the *Grizzly Bears* collection, the 6" "Caledonia" and "McKenzie," looking spiffy in their leather collars.

J.B. Bean & Associates . . . The cream of the crop, the best of the best, are the dignified characters on the Board of Directors. The new year brings about some changes on the board as five new members are

COLLECTOR'S
VALUE GUIDE™

Boyds Plush Overview

introduced: "Dewey P. Wongbruin" (bear), "Grayson R. Hare" (hare), "Walter Q. Fuzzberg" (cat), "Catherine Q. Fuzzberg" (cat) and "Collier P. Hydrant II" (dog).

T.J.'s Best Dressed . . . The Boyds Collection Ltd.'s largest plush series, *T.J.'s Best Dressed,* proves that clothes not only "make the man" but also make the bear, hare, cat, lamb and moose! "Elspethe Ewe" looks ready to frolic in her pink velvet romper and matching bows; "Chamomille Q. Quignapple" appears relaxed in her plaid jumper and matching headband and quilt; "Thayer" is sure to catch any fish in the sea with his bear charm and dapper fisherman's vest and hat; and the green "McShamus O'Growler" is a fashionable Irish token of luck in a soft sweater adorned with clovers.

T.J.'s Best Dressed – Limited Editions . . . Beginning in 1992 with the debut of "Bailey," *T.J.'s Best Dressed – Limited Editions* has grown to include "Emily," "Edmund" and "Matthew," who was recently intro-duced in 1996. Twice a year in the spring and fall, The Boyds Collection Ltd. releases its line of limited edition plush animals, with the exception of "Matthew", who is released in the fall only of each year. Once again, collectors will recognize the familar names Bailey and Matthew, as the names of Boyds creator, Gary Lowenthal's own children. Limited to one year of production, these exquisitely-dressed 8" characters are the elite of the collection and a prized (and difficult) find on the secondary market.

Ornaments . . . There are six new ornaments for 1997, four of which will be released in June, and all of which are heaven-sent. "Stella Goodknight" will usher in sweet dreams while "Regulus P. Roar" will guard you throughout the night. Meanwhile, "Edna May" and "Billy Bob" offer the gifts of love with hearts in hand and matching bows.

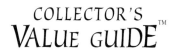

COLLECTOR'S
VALUE GUIDE™

Future Retirements – Plush

Boyds plush retirements are usually announced in *The Boyds Bear Retail Inquirer*. The pieces that are listed below will be retired by December 31st, 1997, expect for those marked with an asterisk, which faced "sudden death retirement" on February 21, 1997. However, some of them will be unavailable before then, depending on when the stock is depleted at The Boyds Collection Ltd. The annual limited edition "Bailey," "Edmund," "Emily" and "Matthew" characters are retired twelve months after their issue. If you've had your eye on any of these plush animals, check with your retailer before it's too late!

Retiring in 1997 . . .

Animal Menagerie
❏ Farland O'Pigg (#5538)

The Archive Series
❏ Alastair (#5725-08)
❏ Anne (#5734)
❏ Camilla (#5732)
❏ Diana (#5738)
❏ Eleanor (#5737-01)
❏ Mary (#5737)

Artisan Series
❏ Edgar (#5864-07)
❏ Farnsworth Jr. (#5870-08)
❏ Hank Krow Jr. (#5865-07)
❏ Higgins (#5877-06)
❏ Higgy (#5876-03)

Bears In The Attic
❏ Dink (#5641-08)
❏ Jethro (#5630)
❏ Reva (#5630-02)
❏ Tipper (#5648-08)

The Choir Bears
❏ Gabriel (#5825)
❏ Joshua (#5826)

Clintons Cabinet
❏ Perry (#1000-11)
❏ Warren (#1002-01)

The Flatties
❏ Lenora Flatstein (#5685-08)

J.B. Bean & Associates
❏ Dufus Bear (#5112)
❏ Otis B. Bean (#5107)

T.J.'s Best Dressed
❏ Aubergine (#9107)
❏ Baaah'b (#9131) *
❏ Carlin Wabbit (#9115)
❏ Demi (#9112)
❏ Emma (#9101)
❏ Hedy (#9186-01)
❏ Marlena (#9154)
❏ Nellie (#91105) *
❏ Puck (#9172)
❏ Stewart Rarebit (#9116)
❏ Tarragon (#9110-07)
❏ Veronica (#9181)

T.J.'s Best Dressed – Limited Editions
❏ Bailey (#9199-05, Spring 1996)
❏ Bailey (#9199-06, Fall 1996)
❏ Emily Babbit (#9150-01, Spring 1996)
❏ Emily Babbit (#9150-05, Fall 1996)
❏ Edmund (#9175-05, Spring 1996)

Ornaments
❏ Angelina (#5615-07)
❏ Gabriella (#7408-08)

Bearfinder – Alphabetical Plush Index

– Key –

If you know the name of your Boyds plush animal, use this alphabetical index (with page and picture numbers) to locate your animal in the value guide section.

– A –

	Page #	Pict #
Abbey Ewe	115	7
Ace Bruin	101	12
Addington	96	3
Alastair	95	15
Alastair & Camilla	92	13
Albert B. Bean	94	8
Aletha The Bearmaker	123	NP
Alexandra	113	16
Alice	110	19
Alice II	96	15
Allison Babbit	112	18
Alouetta de Grizetta	93	4
Amaretto	112	15
Amelia R. Hare	109	12
Amos	104	13
Anastasia	114	NP
Angel Ornaments	123	NP
Angelica	119	13
Angelina	118	2
Anisette	112	16
Anna	113	6
Anne	110	18
Aphrodite	117	16
Aphrodite (w/heart)	117	14
Ansel	92	18
Archer	109	19
Ariel	119	8
Arlo (w/pumpkin pullover)	92	21
Arlo (w/vest)	98	21
Arno-w-ld	107	9
Artemus	87	11
Ashley	112	14
Ashley (musical)	123	NP
Asquith	101	19
Astrid	99	8
Athena	118	5
Attlee	101	1
Aubergine	111	17
Auggie Bruin	100	17
Auntie Adina	123	NP
Auntie Alice	99	9
Auntie Babbit	110	15
Auntie Erma	99	10
Auntie Iola	98	8
Avery B. Bean	102	10

– B –

	Page #	Pict #
Baaah'b	100	20
Babs	111	4
Baby Bear	103	5
Baby Cat	106	12
Baby Hare	114	12
Bailey (w/blue & white dress)	91	NP

– B, cont. –

	Page #	Pict #
Bailey (w/blue dress w/schoolhouse sweater & hat)	91	5
Bailey (w/blue plaid dress & red cape)	91	10
Bailey (w/green tartan plaid dress & hat)	91	16
Bailey (w/navy & cream checkered dress)	91	2
Bailey (w/navy blue sailor dress & hat)	91	13
Bailey (w/purple dress & hat)	91	12
Bailey (w/purple velvet romper, hat & cardigan w/crochet collar)	87	2
Bailey (w/red corduroy dress & hat)	91	7
Bailey (w/spruce green corduroy dress)	91	4
Bailey & Matthew (w/ornaments)	91	17
Bagley Flatberg	107	10
Baldwin	95	9
Barnaby B. Bean	94	18
Bartholemew B. Bean	94	3
Baxter B. Bean	94	19
Bearybear	102	NP
Beatrice Von Hindenmoose	116	12
Bebe (w/cardigan)	116	3
Bebe (w/pullover)	115	16
Becky	98	15
Becky (w/red plaid romper)	92	7
Bedford B. Bean	102	NP
Beecher B. Bunny	110	12
Benjamin	103	NP
Bertha S. Simiansky	116	8
Bertha Utterberg	107	3
Bessie Moostein	106	18
Betty Biscuit	107	15
Betty Lou	123	NP
Big Boy	98	14
Billy Bob	90	1
Billy Ray	97	16
Binkie B. Bear	102	1
Binkie B. Bear II	94	17
Bismark Von Hindenmoose	117	1
Blanche de Bearvoire	92	16
Blinkin	104	5
Bobbie Jo	97	7
Bopper	113	14
Bosley	87	3
Brayburn	108	1
Brewin (#5802)	101	2
Brewin (#5806)	104	2
Brian	90	7
Brie Mouski	115	17
Brigette Delapain	109	21
Brigham Boneah	88	14
Briton R. Hare	114	5
Bronte	105	20
Browning	105	8
Bruce (#1000-08)	96	18
Bruce (#9157-08)	103	NP
Bruce (#98038)	92	5
Bruinhilda Von Bruin	104	NP
Bubba	97	14
Buckley	99	18
Buffington Fitzbruin	88	1
Buffy	97	6
Bumpus	113	15
Bunnylove Rarebit	112	5
Burl	92	6
Busby Bear	123	NP

Bearfinder – Alphabetical Plush Index

Bearfinder – Alphabetical Plush Index

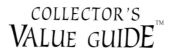

Bearfinder – Alphabetical Plush Index

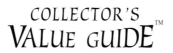

Bearfinder – Alphabetical Plush Index

COLLECTOR'S
VALUE GUIDE™

Bearfinder – Alphabetical Plush Index

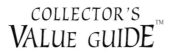

COLLECTOR'S
VALUE GUIDE™

Value Guide – Boyds Plush Animals

How To Use Your Value Guide

This section spotlights the plush animals from The Boyds Collection Ltd. We've collected an extensive list of plush bears and their pictures for this publication, but because The Boyds Collection Ltd. is so prolific and early records are sketchy, there may be bears released before 1991 that are not included here. The plush animals are numbered in the order they are pictured on that page; those listed as "NP" are not pictured. The new 1997 releases are pictured first with previous releases listed after. The plush animals are listed in the following order: *bears, cats, cows, crows, dogs, donkeys, elephants, frogs, gorillas, hares, lambs, lions, mice, monkeys, moose, pigs* and *ornaments*. If you know the name of your plush animal, you can use the *Bearfinder – Alphabetical Plush Index* starting on page 80 to find its location within the value guide.

How To Total The Value Of Your Collection

The value guide is a great way to keep track of the value of your collection. Simply fill in the price you originally paid for your plush animal, then from the "Market Value" column, find the value and record it in the "Value of My Collection" column. All current plush animals are listed with the approximate current retail price. Retired plush are listed with secondary market values. Some retired plush animals have undetermined secondary market values and are listed as "N/E" (not established). To fill in the "Value of My Collection" column for plush animals listed as "N/E," record your purchase price.

You can then total the columns at the bottom of the page (use a pencil so you can change totals as your collection grows) and transfer each subtotal to the summary page at the end of the section to come up with the total value of your collection.

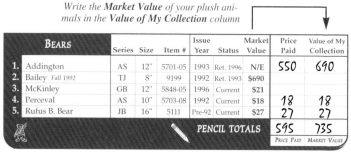

*Write the **Market Value** of your plush animals in the **Value of My Collection** column*

	BEARS	Series	Size	Item #	Issue Year	Status	Market Value	Price Paid	Value of My Collection
1.	Addington	AS	12"	5701-05	1993	Ret. 1996	N/E	550	690
2.	Bailey *Fall 1992*	TJ	8"	9199	1992	Ret. 1993	$690		
3.	McKinley	GB	12"	5848-05	1996	Current	$21		
4.	Perceval	AS	10"	5703-08	1992	Current	$18	18	18
5.	Rufus B. Bear	JB	16"	5111	Pre-92	Current	$27	27	27
					PENCIL TOTALS			595	735
								PRICE PAID	MARKET VALUE

COLLECTOR'S
VALUE GUIDE™

LIMITED EDITION BEARS	Series	Size	Item #	Issue Year	Status	Market Value	Price Paid	Value of My Collection
1. Edmund	TJ	8"	9175-07	1997	Current	**$24**		
2. Bailey	TJ	8"	9199-07	1997	Current	**$27**		
BEARS								
3. Bosley	TJ	8.5"	91561	1997	Current	**$12**		
4. Momma McBear And Delmar	TJ	10"/6"	91007	1997	Current	**$25**		
5. Chamomille Q. Quignapple	TJ	10"	91004	1997	Current	**$24**		
6. Eudemia Q. Quignapple	TJ	9"	91006	1997	Current	**$16**		
7. Caledonia	GB	6"	5840-01	1997	Current	**$9**		
8. McKenzie	GB	6"	5840-03	1997	Current	**$9**		
9. Gwain	TJ	12"	91891-06	1997	Current	**$21**		
10. Ophelia	TJ	16"	91207-01	1997	Current	**$42**		
11. Artemus	CC	8"	1003-08	1997	Current	**$7**		
12. Grace	TJ	10"	91742	1997	Current	**$20**		
13. Hubbard W. Growler	AS	12"	5721-01	1997	Current	**$21**		
14. Grover	TJ	8"	91739	1997	Current	**$12**		
15. Morris	CC	8"	1003-05	1997	Current	**$7**		
16. Twila Higgenthorpe	TJ	6"	91843	1997	Current	**$10**		
17. Tremont	BA	16"	56411-08	1997	Current	**$26**		

✎ **PENCIL TOTALS**

PRICE PAID	MARKET VALUE

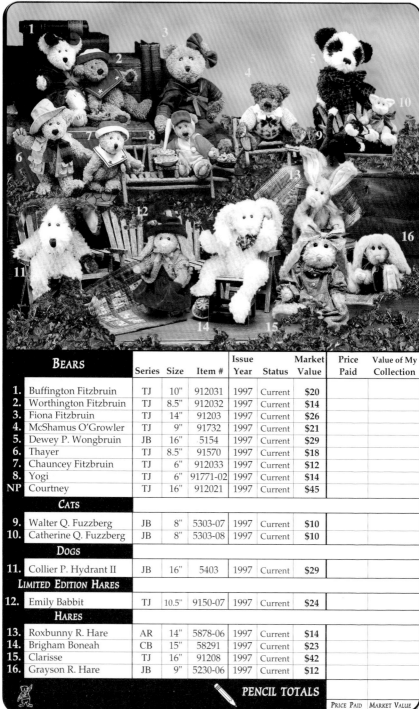

BEARS	Series	Size	Item #	Issue Year	Status	Market Value	Price Paid	Value of My Collection
1. Buffington Fitzbruin	TJ	10"	912031	1997	Current	$20		
2. Worthington Fitzbruin	TJ	8.5"	912032	1997	Current	$14		
3. Fiona Fitzbruin	TJ	14"	91203	1997	Current	$26		
4. McShamus O'Growler	TJ	9"	91732	1997	Current	$21		
5. Dewey P. Wongbruin	JB	16"	5154	1997	Current	$29		
6. Thayer	TJ	8.5"	91570	1997	Current	$18		
7. Chauncey Fitzbruin	TJ	6"	912033	1997	Current	$12		
8. Yogi	TJ	6"	91771-02	1997	Current	$14		
NP Courtney	TJ	16"	912021	1997	Current	$45		
CATS								
9. Walter Q. Fuzzberg	JB	8"	5303-07	1997	Current	$10		
10. Catherine Q. Fuzzberg	JB	8"	5303-08	1997	Current	$10		
DOGS								
11. Collier P. Hydrant II	JB	16"	5403	1997	Current	$29		
LIMITED EDITION HARES								
12. Emily Babbit	TJ	10.5"	9150-07	1997	Current	$24		
HARES								
13. Roxbunny R. Hare	AR	14"	5878-06	1997	Current	$14		
14. Brigham Boneah	CB	15"	58291	1997	Current	$23		
15. Clarisse	TJ	16"	91208	1997	Current	$42		
16. Grayson R. Hare	JB	9"	5230-06	1997	Current	$12		
✎ **PENCIL TOTALS**								
							PRICE PAID	MARKET VALUE

HARES	Series	Size	Item #	Issue Year	Status	Market Value	Price Paid	Value of My Collection
1. Cosette D. Lapine	TJ	10"	916601	1997	Current	$27		
2. Lady Pembrooke	TJ	15"	91892-09	1997	Current	$21		
3. Lucy P. Blumenshine	TJ	6"	91702	1997	Current	$10		
4. Jessica	TJ	8"	9168-02	1997	Current	$12		
5. Lavinia V. Hariweather	TJ	10"	91661	1997	Current	$20		
6. Rose	TJ	7.5"	91112	1997	Current	$12		
7. Hannah	TJ	7.5"	91111	1997	Current	$12		
8. Lucille	TJ	13.5"	91141	1997	Current	$24		
LAMBS								
9. Elspethe Ewe	TJ	8"	91312	1997	Current	$11		
MONKEYS								
10. Finster R. Tsuris	AM	10"	55241-05	1997	Current	$14		
11. Imogene R. Tsuris	AM	10"	55241-11	1997	Current	$14		
PIGS								
12. Kaitlin McSwine	TJ	8"	91601	1997	Current	$12		
13. Primrose II	TJ	11"	9160-01	1997	Current	$20		
14. Lofton Q. McSwine	AM	8"	55391-09	1997	Current	$11		
15. Sheffield O'Swine	AM	8"	55391-07	1997	Current	$11		
			✏ PENCIL TOTALS					
							PRICE PAID	MARKET VALUE

NEW RELEASES

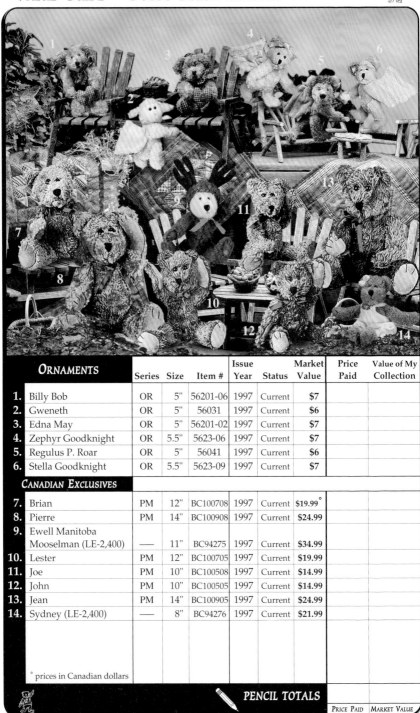

ORNAMENTS	Series	Size	Item #	Issue Year	Status	Market Value	Price Paid	Value of My Collection
1. Billy Bob	OR	5"	56201-06	1997	Current	$7		
2. Gweneth	OR	5"	56031	1997	Current	$6		
3. Edna May	OR	5"	56201-02	1997	Current	$7		
4. Zephyr Goodknight	OR	5.5"	5623-06	1997	Current	$7		
5. Regulus P. Roar	OR	5"	56041	1997	Current	$6		
6. Stella Goodknight	OR	5.5"	5623-09	1997	Current	$7		
CANADIAN EXCLUSIVES								
7. Brian	PM	12"	BC100708	1997	Current	$19.99 °		
8. Pierre	PM	14"	BC100908	1997	Current	$24.99		
9. Ewell Manitoba Mooselman (LE-2,400)	—	11"	BC94275	1997	Current	$34.99		
10. Lester	PM	12"	BC100705	1997	Current	$19.99		
11. Joe	PM	10"	BC100508	1997	Current	$14.99		
12. John	PM	10"	BC100505	1997	Current	$14.99		
13. Jean	PM	14"	BC100905	1997	Current	$24.99		
14. Sydney (LE-2,400)	—	8"	BC94276	1997	Current	$21.99		
° prices in Canadian dollars								

PENCIL TOTALS

PRICE PAID	MARKET VALUE

	BEARS	Series	Size	Item #	Issue Year	Status	Market Value	Price Paid	Value of My Collection
1.	Matthew *Fall 1996*	TJ	8"	91756	1996	Current	**$26**		
2.	Bailey *Spring 1994*	TJ	8"	9199-01	1994	Ret. 1995	**$132**		
3.	Edmund *Spring 1994* • Variation: black & white shirt	TJ	8"	9175-01	1994	Ret. 1995	**$120** **$68**		
4.	Bailey *Fall 1992*	TJ	8"	9199	1992	Ret. 1993	**$690**		
5.	Bailey *Fall 1996*	TJ	8"	9199-06	1996	Current	**$26**		
6.	Edmund *Fall 1996*	TJ	8"	9175-06	1996	Current	**$24**		
7.	Bailey *Fall 1993*	TJ	8"	9170	1993	Ret. 1994	**$230**		
8.	Edmund *Fall 1993*	TJ	8"	9175	1993	Ret. 1994	**$210**		
9.	Edmund *Fall 1994*	TJ	8"	9175-02	1994	Ret. 1995	**$60**		
10.	Bailey *Fall 1994*	TJ	8"	9199-02	1994	Ret. 1995	**$55**		
11.	Edmund *Spring 1996*	TJ	8"	9175-05	1996	Current	**$26**		
12.	Bailey *Spring 1996* • Variation: shiny purple (LE-4,800)	TJ	8"	9199-05	1996	Current	**$26** **$200**		
13.	Bailey *Spring 1995*	TJ	8"	9199-03	1995	Ret. 1996	**$43**		
14.	Edmund *Spring 1995*	TJ	8"	9175-03	1995	Ret. 1996	**$47**		
15.	Edmund *Fall 1995*	TJ	8"	9175-04	1995	Ret. 1996	**$45**		
16.	Bailey *Fall 1995*	TJ	8"	9199-04	1995	Ret. 1996	**$57**		
17.	Bailey & Matthew *Fall 1996* (w/2 Bearstone ornaments)	TJ	8"	9224	1996	Ret. 1996	**$70**		
NP	Bailey *Spring 1993*	TJ	8"	N/A	1993	Ret. 1994	**$270**		
						PENCIL TOTALS			
								PRICE PAID	MARKET VALUE

BEARS

VALUE GUIDE – BOYDS PLUSH ANIMALS

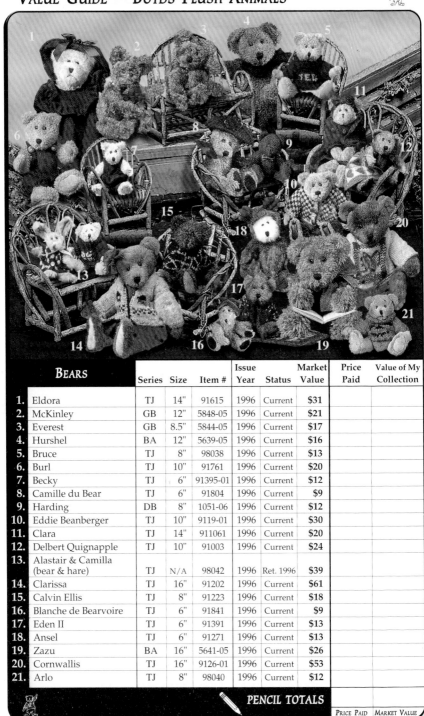

BEARS	Series	Size	Item #	Issue Year	Status	Market Value	Price Paid	Value of My Collection
1. Eldora	TJ	14"	91615	1996	Current	$31		
2. McKinley	GB	12"	5848-05	1996	Current	$21		
3. Everest	GB	8.5"	5844-05	1996	Current	$17		
4. Hurshel	BA	12"	5639-05	1996	Current	$16		
5. Bruce	TJ	8"	98038	1996	Current	$13		
6. Burl	TJ	10"	91761	1996	Current	$20		
7. Becky	TJ	6"	91395-01	1996	Current	$12		
8. Camille du Bear	TJ	6"	91804	1996	Current	$9		
9. Harding	DB	8"	1051-06	1996	Current	$12		
10. Eddie Beanberger	TJ	10"	9119-01	1996	Current	$30		
11. Clara	TJ	14"	911061	1996	Current	$20		
12. Delbert Quignapple	TJ	10"	91003	1996	Current	$24		
13. Alastair & Camilla (bear & hare)	TJ	N/A	98042	1996	Ret. 1996	$39		
14. Clarissa	TJ	16"	91202	1996	Current	$61		
15. Calvin Ellis	TJ	8"	91223	1996	Current	$18		
16. Blanche de Bearvoire	TJ	6"	91841	1996	Current	$9		
17. Eden II	TJ	6"	91391	1996	Current	$13		
18. Ansel	TJ	6"	91271	1996	Current	$13		
19. Zazu	BA	16"	5641-05	1996	Current	$26		
20. Cornwallis	TJ	16"	9126-01	1996	Current	$53		
21. Arlo	TJ	8"	98040	1996	Current	$12		

PENCIL TOTALS

Price Paid	Market Value

BEARS	Series	Size	Item #	Issue Year	Status	Market Value	Price Paid	Value of My Collection
1. Isaiah	TJ	10"	917304	1996	Current	$19		
2. Corinna	TJ	16"	91201	1996	Current	$45		
3. Guinevere	TJ	12"	91891-09	1996	Current	$21		
4. Alouetta de Grizetta	TJ	6"	91842	1996	Current	$9		
5. Rex	TJ	8"	912440	1996	Current	$18		
6. Louella	TJ	10"	91242	1996	Current	$24		
7. Federico	TJ	11"	98039	1996	Current	$21		
8. Roxanne K. Bear	TJ	10"	91741	1996	Current	$20		
9. Geraldo	TJ	8"	912441	1996	Current	$19		
10. Sandy Claus	TJ	16"	91731	1995	Current	$31		
11. Newton	TJ	8"	9133	1994	Ret. 1996	$45		
12. Lizzie McBee	TJ	8"	91005	1996	Current	$20		
13. Huck	TJ	6"	918051	1996	Current	$12		
14. Lars	TJ	8"	91735	1996	Current	$18		
15. Erin K. Bear	TJ	7"	91562	1996	Current	$11		
16. Niki	TJ	6"	91730	1996	Current	$13		
17. Ewell	TJ	8"	9127	1994	Current	$17		
18. Walton	TJ	11"	9128	1994	Current	$21		
19. Ophelia W. Witebred	TJ	16"	91207	1996	Current	$42		
20. Emmett Elfberg	TJ	10"	917305	1996	Current	$21		

BEARS

PENCIL TOTALS

PRICE PAID	MARKET VALUE

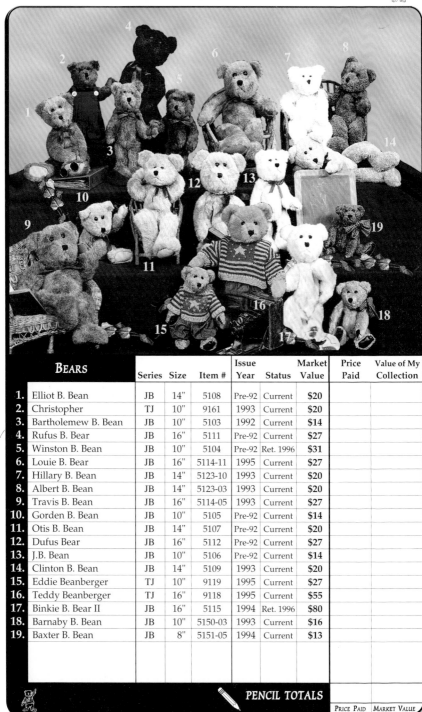

BEARS		Series	Size	Item #	Issue Year	Status	Market Value	Price Paid	Value of My Collection
1.	Elliot B. Bean	JB	14"	5108	Pre-92	Current	**$20**		
2.	Christopher	TJ	10"	9161	1993	Current	**$20**		
3.	Bartholemew B. Bean	JB	10"	5103	1992	Current	**$14**		
4.	Rufus B. Bear	JB	16"	5111	Pre-92	Current	**$27**		
5.	Winston B. Bean	JB	10"	5104	Pre-92	Ret. 1996	**$31**		
6.	Louie B. Bear	JB	16"	5114-11	1995	Current	**$27**		
7.	Hillary B. Bean	JB	14"	5123-10	1993	Current	**$20**		
8.	Albert B. Bean	JB	14"	5123-03	1993	Current	**$20**		
9.	Travis B. Bean	JB	16"	5114-05	1993	Current	**$27**		
10.	Gorden B. Bean	JB	10"	5105	Pre-92	Current	**$14**		
11.	Otis B. Bean	JB	14"	5107	Pre-92	Current	**$20**		
12.	Dufus Bear	JB	16"	5112	Pre-92	Current	**$27**		
13.	J.B. Bean	JB	10"	5106	Pre-92	Current	**$14**		
14.	Clinton B. Bean	JB	14"	5109	1993	Current	**$20**		
15.	Eddie Beanberger	TJ	10"	9119	1995	Current	**$27**		
16.	Teddy Beanberger	TJ	16"	9118	1995	Current	**$55**		
17.	Binkie B. Bear II	JB	16"	5115	1994	Ret. 1996	**$80**		
18.	Barnaby B. Bean	JB	10"	5150-03	1993	Current	**$16**		
19.	Baxter B. Bean	JB	8"	5151-05	1994	Current	**$13**		

PENCIL TOTALS

PRICE PAID	MARKET VALUE

BEARS		Series	Size	Item #	Issue Year	Status	Market Value	Price Paid	Value of My Collection
1.	Churchill	AS	12"	5700	Pre-92	Current	$20		
2.	Raleigh	AS	10"	5703M	1994	Current	$18		
3.	Spencer	AS	5.5"	5725	1993	Current	$7		
4.	Neville	AS	5.5"	5707	Pre-92	Current	$7		
5.	Malcolm	AS	16"	5711	1992	Current	$33		
6.	Callaghan	AS	8"	5704	Pre-92	Ret. 1996	$50		
7.	Lancelot	AS	21"	5722-11	1996	Current	$55		
8.	Heath II	AS	10"	5703N	1992	Current	$18		
9.	Baldwin	AS	5.5"	5718	1992	Current	$7		
10.	Whitaker Q. Bruin	TJ	5.5"	91806	1996	Current	$11		
11.	Eden	AS	5.5"	5708	Pre-92	Ret. 1996	$32		
12.	Cecil	AS	5.5"	5726	1993	Ret. 1996	$21		
13.	Thatcher	AS	5.5"	5706	Pre-92	Current	$7		
14.	Percy	AS	5.5"	5725-11	1994	Current	$7		
15.	Alastair	AS	5.5"	5725-08	1995	Current	$7		
16.	Grenville	AS	16"	5715	1992	Current	$33		
17.	Macmillan	AS	8"	5705-10	1995	Current	$13		
18.	Wilson	AS	8"	5705	Pre-92	Current	$13		
19.	Walpole	AS	8"	5705M	1993	Current	$13		
20.	Jefferson	DB	8"	1050-02	1995	Ret. 1996	$27		
21.	Hancock	DB	8"	1050-11	1995	Ret. 1996	$32		

BEARS

PENCIL TOTALS

PRICE PAID	MARKET VALUE

BEARS	Series	Size	Item #	Issue Year	Status	Market Value	Price Paid	Value of My Collection
1. Smith Witter II	JB	17"	5110	1994	Current	$29		
2. Eugenia (w/apples)	TJ	16"	9120-01	1994	Ret. 1995	$84		
3. Addington	AS	12"	5701-05	1993	Ret. 1996	N/E		
4. Essex	AS	12"	5701-10	1994	Ret. 1996	N/E		
5. Franklin	DB	8"	1050-06	1995	Ret. 1995	$27		
6. Warren	CC	8"	1002-01	1993	Current	$7		
7. Humboldt	GB	6"	5840-05	1996	Current	$9		
8. Perceval	AS	10"	5703-08	1992	Current	$18		
9. Tyler Summerfield	TJ	12"	9124	1996	Current	$39		
10. Matthew H. Growler	AS	12"	5721	1996	Current	$21		
11. Dexter	TJ	8"	91331	1996	Current	$25		
12. Wellington	AS	21"	5722	1992	Current	$55		
13. Leon	CC	8"	1001-08	1993	Current	$7		
14. Perry	CC	8"	1000-11	1994	Current	$6		
15. Alice II	CC	11"	1101-08	1995	Current	$12		
16. Hazel	CC	8"	1000-03	1993	Ret. 1996	$22		
17. Federico	CC	11"	1100-08	1993	Current	$10		
18. Bruce	CC	8"	1000-08	1993	Current	$6		
19. George	CC	11"	1100-03	1996	Current	$10		
20. Vincent	CC	11"	1100-11	1995	Current	$10		

PENCIL TOTALS

	Price Paid	Market Value

BEARS				Issue		Market	Price	Value of My
	Series	Size	Item #	Year	Status	Value	Paid	Collection
1. Chan	TJ	6"	9153	1994	Current	$13		
2. Watson	TJ	8"	9187	1993	Current	$17		
3. Sherlock	TJ	11"	9188	1992	Current	$21		
4. John	CB	13"	5828	1992	Current	$20		
5. Skip	BA	12"	5638	1992	Ret. 1996	N/E		
6. Buffy	BA	12"	5639-10	1995	Ret. 1996	N/E		
7. Bobbie Jo	BB	12"	5853	1992	Current	$20		
8. Joshua	CB	9"	5826	1992	Current	$14		
9. Gabriel	CB	9"	5825	1992	Current	$14		
10. Winkie II	BA	12"	5639-08	1995	Current	$16		
11. Kip	BA	8"	5642-08	1993	Current	$11		
12. Missy	BA	8"	5642-10	1995	Ret. 1996	$25		
13. Chipper	BA	8"	5642-05	1996	Current	$11		
14. Bubba	BB	16"	5856	1992	Current	$27		
15. Elly Mae	BB	9"	5850-10	1995	Current	$14		
16. Billy Ray	BB	9"	5850	1992	Current	$14		
17. Jody	BA	16"	5641-09	1995	Ret. 1996	N/E		
18. Hockley	BA	16"	5640	1992	Ret. 1996	$38		
19. Sebastian	CB	13"	5827	1992	Current	$20		
20. Dink	BA	16"	5641-08	1995	Current	$24		
				✏ PENCIL TOTALS				
							Price Paid	Market Value

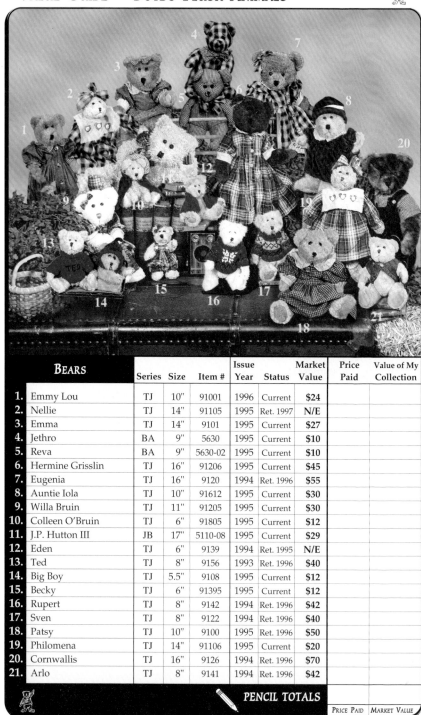

BEARS		Series	Size	Item #	Issue Year	Status	Market Value	Price Paid	Value of My Collection
1.	Emmy Lou	TJ	10"	91001	1996	Current	$24		
2.	Nellie	TJ	14"	91105	1995	Ret. 1997	N/E		
3.	Emma	TJ	14"	9101	1995	Current	$27		
4.	Jethro	BA	9"	5630	1995	Current	$10		
5.	Reva	BA	9"	5630-02	1995	Current	$10		
6.	Hermine Grisslin	TJ	16"	91206	1995	Current	$45		
7.	Eugenia	TJ	16"	9120	1994	Ret. 1996	$55		
8.	Auntie Iola	TJ	10"	91612	1995	Current	$30		
9.	Willa Bruin	TJ	11"	91205	1995	Current	$30		
10.	Colleen O'Bruin	TJ	6"	91805	1995	Current	$12		
11.	J.P. Hutton III	JB	17"	5110-08	1995	Current	$29		
12.	Eden	TJ	6"	9139	1994	Ret. 1995	N/E		
13.	Ted	TJ	8"	9156	1993	Ret. 1996	$40		
14.	Big Boy	TJ	5.5"	9108	1995	Current	$12		
15.	Becky	TJ	6"	91395	1995	Current	$12		
16.	Rupert	TJ	8"	9142	1994	Ret. 1996	$42		
17.	Sven	TJ	8"	9122	1994	Ret. 1996	$40		
18.	Patsy	TJ	10"	9100	1995	Ret. 1996	$50		
19.	Philomena	TJ	14"	91106	1995	Current	$20		
20.	Cornwallis	TJ	16"	9126	1994	Ret. 1996	$70		
21.	Arlo	TJ	8"	9141	1994	Ret. 1996	$42		

✏️ **PENCIL TOTALS**

Price Paid	Market Value

	BEARS	Series	Size	Item #	Issue Year	Status	Market Value	Price Paid	Value of My Collection
1.	Olaf	TJ	12"	9138	1994	Ret. 1996	$76		
2.	Nicholas	TJ	8"	9173	1993	Current	$20		
3.	Cavendish	AS	12"	5701-02	1994	Ret. 1996	$43		
4.	Harrison	TJ	10"	9176	1993	Current	$20		
5.	Claire	TJ	10"	9179	1994	Current	$20		
6.	Skidoo	TJ	11"	9193	1992	Current	$24		
7.	Gunnar	TJ	8"	9123	1995	Ret. 1996	$32		
8.	Astrid	TJ	9"	9137	1994	Ret. 1996	N/E		
9.	Auntie Alice	TJ	10"	9183	1992	Ret. 1996	$39		
10.	Auntie Erma	TJ	10"	91832	1996	Current	$21		
11.	Mistle	JB	8.5"	5151-04	1994	Current	$13	✓	
12.	Toe	JB	8.5"	5151-02	1994	Current	$13		
13.	Chanel de la Plumtete	TJ	6"	9184	1995	Current	$9		
14.	Elgin	TJ	6.5"	9129	1994	Current	$13		
15.	Simone de Bearvoire	TJ	6"	9180	1993	Ret. 1996	$27		
16.	Slugger	TJ	8"	9177-01	1996	Current	$26		
17.	Christian	TJ	8"	9190	1992	Current	$18		
18.	Buckley	TJ	8"	9104	1995	Ret. 1996	N/E		
19.	Lydia	TJ	14"	9182	1993	Ret. 1996	$48		
NP	Roosevelt	TJ	8"	9902	1995	Ret. 1996	$32		

PENCIL TOTALS

PRICE PAID	MARKET VALUE

BEARS

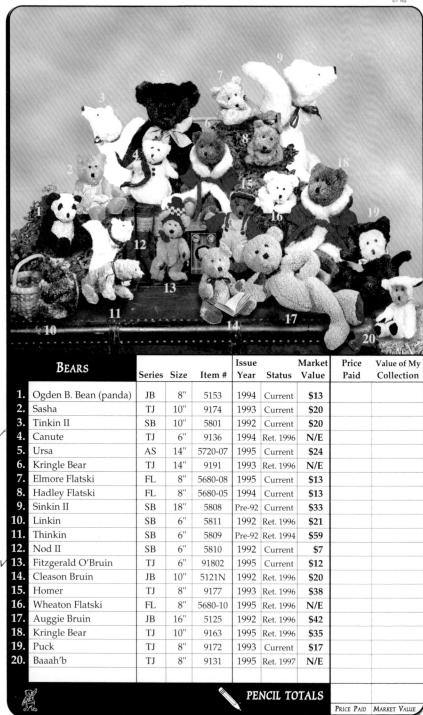

	BEARS	Series	Size	Item #	Issue Year	Status	Market Value	Price Paid	Value of My Collection
1.	Ogden B. Bean (panda)	JB	8"	5153	1994	Current	$13		
2.	Sasha	TJ	10"	9174	1993	Current	$20		
3.	Tinkin II	SB	10"	5801	1992	Current	$20		
4.	Canute	TJ	6"	9136	1994	Ret. 1996	N/E		
5.	Ursa	AS	14"	5720-07	1995	Current	$24		
6.	Kringle Bear	TJ	14"	9191	1993	Ret. 1996	N/E		
7.	Elmore Flatski	FL	8"	5680-08	1995	Current	$13		
8.	Hadley Flatski	FL	8"	5680-05	1994	Current	$13		
9.	Sinkin II	SB	18"	5808	Pre-92	Current	$33		
10.	Linkin	SB	6"	5811	1992	Ret. 1996	$21		
11.	Thinkin	SB	6"	5809	Pre-92	Ret. 1994	$59		
12.	Nod II	SB	6"	5810	1992	Current	$7		
13.	Fitzgerald O'Bruin	TJ	6"	91802	1995	Current	$12		
14.	Cleason Bruin	JB	10"	5121N	1992	Ret. 1996	$20		
15.	Homer	TJ	8"	9177	1993	Ret. 1996	$38		
16.	Wheaton Flatski	FL	8"	5680-10	1995	Ret. 1996	N/E		
17.	Auggie Bruin	JB	16"	5125	1992	Ret. 1996	$42		
18.	Kringle Bear	TJ	10"	9163	1995	Ret. 1996	$35		
19.	Puck	TJ	8"	9172	1993	Current	$17		
20.	Baaah'b	TJ	8"	9131	1995	Ret. 1997	N/E		

PENCIL TOTALS

PRICE PAID	MARKET VALUE

	BEARS	Series	Size	Item #	Issue Year	Status	Market Value	Price Paid	Value of My Collection
1.	Attlee	AS	8"	5705B	1992	Ret. 1993	**$94**		
2.	Brewin	SB	10"	5802	Pre-92	Ret. 1995	**$51**		
3.	Major II	AS	10"	5703B	1992	Ret. 1996	**N/E**		
4.	Lem Bruin	JB	14"	5123	Pre-92	Ret. 1994	**$54**		
5.	Rudolf	SB	18"	5807B	1992	Ret. 1992	**$280**		
6.	Gunther Von Bruin	WB	6"	5012	1993	Ret. 1993	**$64**		
7.	Gladstone	AS	12"	5701	Pre-92	Ret. 1993	**$85**		
8.	Snowball	JB	14"	5123W	1992	Ret. 1993	**$57**		
9.	Melbourne	AS	12"	5719	1992	Ret. 1994	**$53**		
10.	Werner Von Bruin	WB	6"	5010-11	1993	Ret. 1995	**$38**		
11.	Moriarity	TJ	11"	9171	1993	Ret. 1996	**$52**		
12.	Ace Bruin	JB	10"	5122	Pre-92	Ret. 1996	**$33**		
13.	Disreali	AS	5.5"	5716	Pre-92	Ret. 1992	**$57**		
14.	Otto Von Bruin	WB	6"	5010	1992	Ret. 1994	**$34**		
15.	Geneva	TJ	8"	9162	1993	Ret. 1994	**$86**		
16.	Theodore	TJ	7.5"	9196	1992	Ret. 1994	**N/E**		
17.	Coco Bruin	JB	10"	5121	1992	Ret. 1996	**$44**		
18.	Winkin	SB	10"	5800	Pre-92	Ret. 1993	**$56**		
19.	Asquith	AS	8"	5705-05	1993	Ret. 1996	**$36**		
20.	Pop Bruin	JB	16"	5124	Pre-92	Ret. 1996	**$51**		
21.	Fritz Von Bruin	WB	6"	5014	1992	Ret. 1993	**$32**		

✏️ PENCIL TOTALS

PRICE PAID	MARKET VALUE

BEARS

BEARS	Series	Size	Item #	Issue Year	Status	Market Value	Price Paid	Value of My Collection
1. Binkie B. Bear	JB	16"	5115	Pre-92	Ret. 1993	**$78**		
2. Sniffles	HD	9"	5773	Pre-92	Ret. 1992	**$105**		
3. Homer	HD	14"	5760	Pre-92	Ret. 1993	**$130**		
4. Phillip Bear Hop	TJ	11"	9189	1992	Ret. 1992	**$215**		
5. Daryl Bear	JB	16"	5114	Pre-92	Ret. 1993	**N/E**		
6. Winkie II	BA	12"	5639	1993	Ret. 1994	**N/E**		
7. Pohley	HD	9"	5768	Pre-92	Ret. 1993	**$90**		
8. Buzz B. Bean	JB	N/A	5120	Pre-92	Retired	**N/E**		
9. Sherlock	AS	11"	5821	1992	Ret. 1992	**$44**		
10. Avery B. Bean	JB	N/A	5101	Pre-92	Retired	**N/E**		
11. Dink	BA	16"	5641	1992	Ret. 1994	**N/E**		
12. Milo	HD	9"	5767	1992	Ret. 1994	**$80**		
13. Grumps	HD	9"	5766	Pre-92	Ret. 1994	**$76**		
14. Jesse	CC	11"	1100-05	1993	Ret. 1996	**$31**		
15. Henry	CC	8"	1000-05	1993	Ret. 1996	**$32**		
16. Scooter	BA	8"	5642-03	1993	Ret. 1995	**N/E**		
17. Honeypot	HD	14"	5761	Pre-92	Ret. 1993	**$138**		
18. Fitzroy	TJ	7.5"	9195	1992	Ret. 1994	**N/E**		
NP Bearybear	HD	14"	5762	1992	Ret. 1994	**$165**		
NP Bedford B. Bean	JB	N/A	5121-08	Pre-92	Retired	**N/E**		
NP Mohley	HD	9"	5771	Pre-92	Retired	**$95**		
					PENCIL TOTALS			
							PRICE PAID	MARKET VALUE

BEARS		Series	Size	Item #	Issue Year	Status	Market Value	Price Paid	Value of My Collection
1.	Nana	HD	14"	5765	Pre-92	Ret. 1991	**$315**		
2.	Lacy Bear	TJ	14"	6101DB	Pre-92	Ret. 1992	**$113**		
3.	Lacy Bear	TJ	10"	6100DB	Pre-92	Ret. 1992	**$100**		
4.	Fleurette	TJ	12"	6103B	Pre-92	Ret. 1991	**$115**		
5.	Baby Bear	TJ	10"	6105B	Pre-92	Ret. 1991	**$60**		
6.	Gramps	HD	18"	5770	Pre-92	Ret. 1991	**$190**		
7.	Gram	HD	18"	5775	Pre-92	Ret. 1991	**$190**		
8.	Rohley	HD	9"	5769	Pre-92	Ret. 1991	**$98**		
9.	Squeekie Bear	SQ	8"	5616	1992	Ret. 1992	**$82**		
10.	Lacy Bear	TJ	14"	6101B	Pre-92	Ret. 1992	**$113**		
11.	Squeeky Bear	SQ	8"	5615	Pre-92	Ret. 1991	**N/E**		
12.	Royce Bear	TJ	14"	6107B	Pre-92	Ret. 1991	**$112**		
NP	Benjamin	TJ	10"	9159	1993	Ret. 1994	**N/E**		
NP	Bruce	TJ	8"	9157-08	1993	Ret. 1994	**N/E**		
NP	Mickey	TJ	8"	9157-01	1993	Ret. 1994	**N/E**		
NP	Patrick	TJ	8"	9901	1995	Ret. 1995	**$54**		

BEARS

 PENCIL TOTALS

PRICE PAID	MARKET VALUE

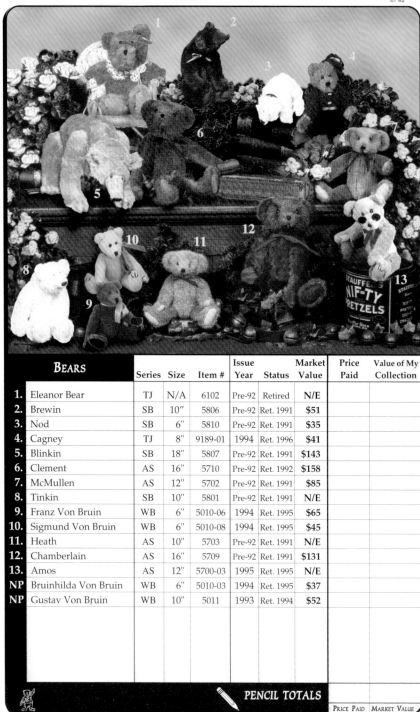

	BEARS	Series	Size	Item #	Issue Year	Status	Market Value	Price Paid	Value of My Collection
1.	Eleanor Bear	TJ	N/A	6102	Pre-92	Retired	N/E		
2.	Brewin	SB	10"	5806	Pre-92	Ret. 1991	$51		
3.	Nod	SB	6"	5810	Pre-92	Ret. 1991	$35		
4.	Cagney	TJ	8"	9189-01	1994	Ret. 1996	$41		
5.	Blinkin	SB	18"	5807	Pre-92	Ret. 1991	$143		
6.	Clement	AS	16"	5710	Pre-92	Ret. 1992	$158		
7.	McMullen	AS	12"	5702	Pre-92	Ret. 1991	$85		
8.	Tinkin	SB	10"	5801	Pre-92	Ret. 1991	N/E		
9.	Franz Von Bruin	WB	6"	5010-06	1994	Ret. 1995	$65		
10.	Sigmund Von Bruin	WB	6"	5010-08	1994	Ret. 1995	$45		
11.	Heath	AS	10"	5703	Pre-92	Ret. 1991	N/E		
12.	Chamberlain	AS	16"	5709	Pre-92	Ret. 1991	$131		
13.	Amos	AS	12"	5700-03	1995	Ret. 1995	N/E		
NP	Bruinhilda Von Bruin	WB	6"	5010-03	1994	Ret. 1995	$37		
NP	Gustav Von Bruin	WB	10"	5011	1993	Ret. 1994	$52		

PENCIL TOTALS

Price Paid	Market Value

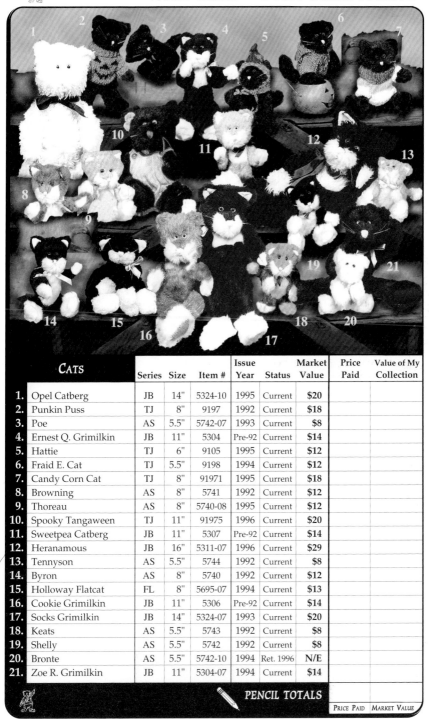

	CATS	Series	Size	Item #	Issue Year	Status	Market Value	Price Paid	Value of My Collection
1.	Opel Catberg	JB	14"	5324-10	1995	Current	$20		
2.	Punkin Puss	TJ	8"	9197	1992	Current	$18		
3.	Poe	AS	5.5"	5742-07	1993	Current	$8		
4.	Ernest Q. Grimilkin	JB	11"	5304	Pre-92	Current	$14		
5.	Hattie	TJ	6"	9105	1995	Current	$12		
6.	Fraid E. Cat	TJ	5.5"	9198	1994	Current	$12		
7.	Candy Corn Cat	TJ	8"	91971	1995	Current	$18		
8.	Browning	AS	8"	5741	1992	Current	$12		
9.	Thoreau	AS	8"	5740-08	1995	Current	$12		
10.	Spooky Tangaween	TJ	11"	91975	1996	Current	$20		
11.	Sweetpea Catberg	JB	11"	5307	Pre-92	Current	$14		
12.	Heranamous	JB	16"	5311-07	1996	Current	$29		
13.	Tennyson	AS	5.5"	5744	1992	Current	$8		
14.	Byron	AS	8"	5740	1992	Current	$12		
15.	Holloway Flatcat	FL	8"	5695-07	1994	Current	$13		
16.	Cookie Grimilkin	JB	11"	5306	Pre-92	Current	$14		
17.	Socks Grimilkin	JB	14"	5324-07	1993	Current	$20		
18.	Keats	AS	5.5"	5743	1992	Current	$8		
19.	Shelly	AS	5.5"	5742	1992	Current	$8		
20.	Bronte	AS	5.5"	5742-10	1994	Ret. 1996	N/E		
21.	Zoe R. Grimilkin	JB	11"	5304-07	1994	Current	$14		
					✏️ PENCIL TOTALS				
								Price Paid	Market Value

CATS

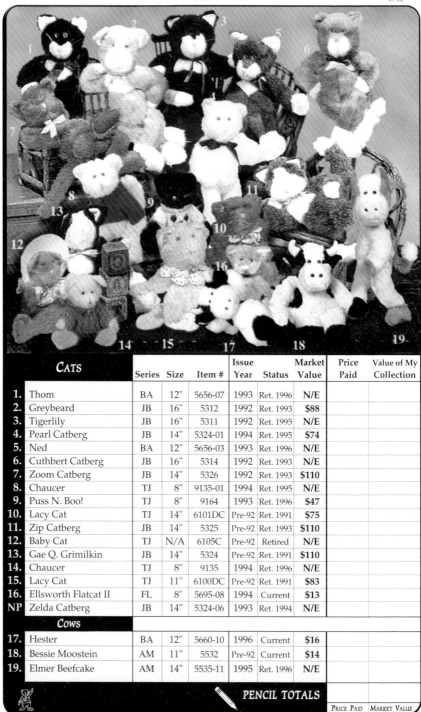

	CATS	Series	Size	Item #	Issue Year	Status	Market Value	Price Paid	Value of My Collection
1.	Thom	BA	12"	5656-07	1993	Ret. 1996	N/E		
2.	Greybeard	JB	16"	5312	1992	Ret. 1993	$88		
3.	Tigerlily	JB	16"	5311	1992	Ret. 1995	N/E		
4.	Pearl Catberg	JB	14"	5324-01	1994	Ret. 1995	$74		
5.	Ned	BA	12"	5656-03	1993	Ret. 1996	N/E		
6.	Cuthbert Catberg	JB	16"	5314	1992	Ret. 1993	N/E		
7.	Zoom Catberg	JB	14"	5326	1992	Ret. 1993	$110		
8.	Chaucer	TJ	8"	9135-01	1994	Ret. 1995	N/E		
9.	Puss N. Boo!	TJ	8"	9164	1993	Ret. 1996	$47		
10.	Lacy Cat	TJ	14"	6101DC	Pre-92	Ret. 1991	$75		
11.	Zip Catberg	JB	14"	5325	Pre-92	Ret. 1993	$110		
12.	Baby Cat	TJ	N/A	6105C	Pre-92	Retired	N/E		
13.	Gae Q. Grimilkin	JB	14"	5324	Pre-92	Ret. 1991	$110		
14.	Chaucer	TJ	8"	9135	1994	Ret. 1996	N/E		
15.	Lacy Cat	TJ	11"	6100DC	Pre-92	Ret. 1991	$83		
16.	Ellsworth Flatcat II	FL	8"	5695-08	1994	Current	$13		
NP	Zelda Catberg	JB	14"	5324-06	1993	Ret. 1994	N/E		
	COWS								
17.	Hester	BA	12"	5660-10	1996	Current	$16		
18.	Bessie Moostein	AM	11"	5532	Pre-92	Current	$14		
19.	Elmer Beefcake	AM	14"	5535-11	1995	Ret. 1996	N/E		

PENCIL TOTALS

Price Paid	Market Value

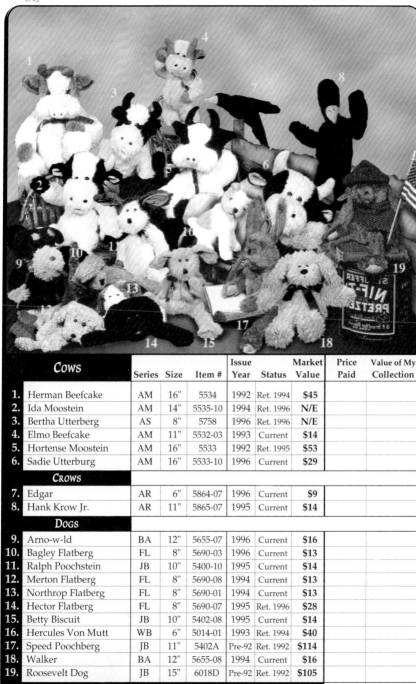

COWS	Series	Size	Item #	Issue Year	Status	Market Value	Price Paid	Value of My Collection
1. Herman Beefcake	AM	16"	5534	1992	Ret. 1994	**$45**		
2. Ida Moostein	AM	14"	5535-10	1994	Ret. 1996	**N/E**		
3. Bertha Utterberg	AS	8"	5758	1996	Ret. 1996	**N/E**		
4. Elmo Beefcake	AM	11"	5532-03	1993	Current	**$14**		
5. Hortense Moostein	AM	16"	5533	1992	Ret. 1995	**$53**		
6. Sadie Utterburg	AM	16"	5533-10	1996	Current	**$29**		
CROWS								
7. Edgar	AR	6"	5864-07	1996	Current	**$9**		
8. Hank Krow Jr.	AR	11"	5865-07	1995	Current	**$14**		
DOGS								
9. Arno-w-ld	BA	12"	5655-07	1996	Current	**$16**		
10. Bagley Flatberg	FL	8"	5690-03	1996	Current	**$13**		
11. Ralph Poochstein	JB	10"	5400-10	1995	Current	**$14**		
12. Merton Flatberg	FL	8"	5690-08	1994	Current	**$13**		
13. Northrop Flatberg	FL	8"	5690-01	1994	Current	**$13**		
14. Hector Flatberg	FL	8"	5690-07	1995	Ret. 1996	**$28**		
15. Betty Biscuit	JB	10"	5402-08	1995	Current	**$14**		
16. Hercules Von Mutt	WB	6"	5014-01	1993	Ret. 1994	**$40**		
17. Speed Poochberg	JB	11"	5402A	Pre-92	Ret. 1992	**$114**		
18. Walker	BA	12"	5655-08	1994	Current	**$16**		
19. Roosevelt Dog	JB	15"	6018D	Pre-92	Ret. 1992	**$105**		
				PENCIL TOTALS			Price Paid	Market Value

COWS/CROWS/DOGS

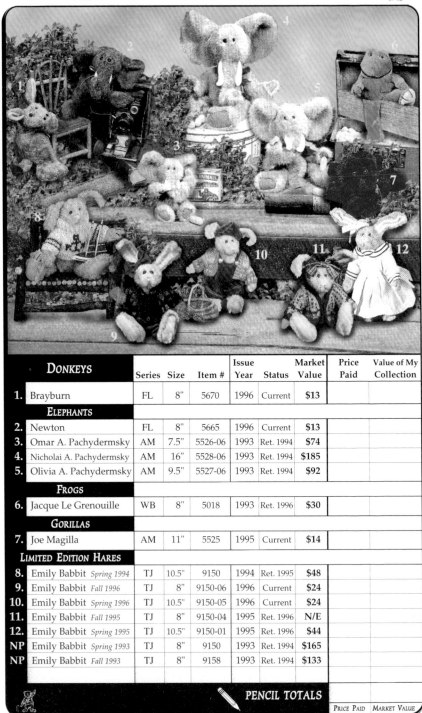

	DONKEYS	Series	Size	Item #	Issue Year	Status	Market Value	Price Paid	Value of My Collection
1.	Brayburn	FL	8"	5670	1996	Current	**$13**		
	ELEPHANTS								
2.	Newton	FL	8"	5665	1996	Current	**$13**		
3.	Omar A. Pachydermsky	AM	7.5"	5526-06	1993	Ret. 1994	**$74**		
4.	Nicholai A. Pachydermsky	AM	16"	5528-06	1993	Ret. 1994	**$185**		
5.	Olivia A. Pachydermsky	AM	9.5"	5527-06	1993	Ret. 1994	**$92**		
	FROGS								
6.	Jacque Le Grenouille	WB	8"	5018	1993	Ret. 1996	**$30**		
	GORILLAS								
7.	Joe Magilla	AM	11"	5525	1995	Current	**$14**		
	LIMITED EDITION HARES								
8.	Emily Babbit *Spring 1994*	TJ	10.5"	9150	1994	Ret. 1995	**$48**		
9.	Emily Babbit *Fall 1996*	TJ	8"	9150-06	1996	Current	**$24**		
10.	Emily Babbit *Spring 1996*	TJ	10.5"	9150-05	1996	Current	**$24**		
11.	Emily Babbit *Fall 1995*	TJ	8"	9150-04	1995	Ret. 1996	**N/E**		
12.	Emily Babbit *Spring 1995*	TJ	10.5"	9150-01	1995	Ret. 1996	**$44**		
NP	Emily Babbit *Spring 1993*	TJ	8"	9150	1993	Ret. 1994	**$165**		
NP	Emily Babbit *Fall 1993*	TJ	8"	9158	1993	Ret. 1994	**$133**		

PENCIL TOTALS

PRICE PAID	MARKET VALUE

	HARES	Series	Size	Item #	Issue Year	Status	Market Value	Price Paid	Value of My Collection
1.	Priscilla R. Hare	JB	14"	5217-08	1993	Current	$20		
2.	Chelsea R. Hare	JB	14"	5217-01	1993	Current	$20		
3.	Chloe Fitzhare	JB	17"	5240-03	1996	Current	$29		
4.	Elizabeth	TJ	7.5"	98041	1996	Ret. 1996	N/E		
5.	Lily R. Hare	JB	8"	5227-01	1994	Current	$10		
6.	Eloise R. Hare	JB	8.5"	5230-10	1994	Current	$12		
7.	Zelda Fitzhare	JB	17"	5240-10	1995	Current	$29		
8.	Daphne R. Hare	JB	14"	5225	1992	Current	$20		
9.	Livingston R. Hare	JB	12"	5200	Pre-92	Current	$14		
10.	Clara R. Hare	JB	8"	5227-08	1994	Current	$10		
11.	Stanley R. Hare	JB	12"	5201	1992	Current	$14		
12.	Amelia R. Hare	JB	12"	5203	Pre-92	Current	$14		
13.	Harriett R. Hare	JB	12"	5200-08	1994	Ret. 1996	N/E		
14.	G.G. Willikers	TJ	8"	91162	1996	Current	$20		
15.	Charlotte R. Hare	JB	14"	5224	1992	Current	$20		
16.	Marlena	TJ	10.5"	9154	1994	Current	$20		
17.	Emma R. Hare	JB	14"	5225-08	1994	Ret. 1995	N/E		
18.	Chesterfield Q. Burpee	TJ	8"	91546	1996	Current	$21		
19.	Archer	TJ	10"	91544	1996	Current	$24		
20.	Diana	TJ	8"	9181-01	1996	Current	$21		
21.	Brigette Delapain	TJ	10"	91691	1996	Current	$21		

PENCIL TOTALS

Price Paid	Market Value

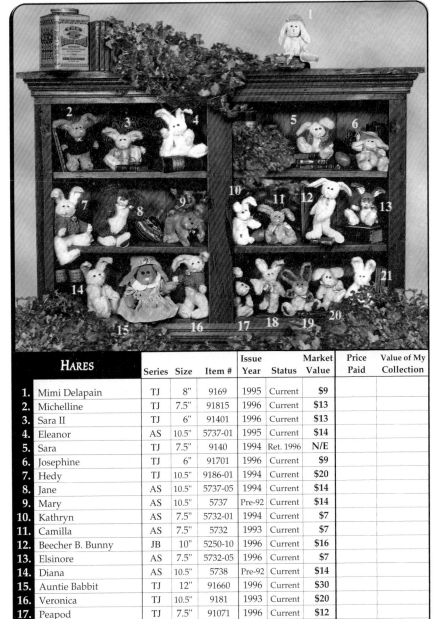

	HARES	Series	Size	Item #	Issue Year	Status	Market Value	Price Paid	Value of My Collection
1.	Mimi Delapain	TJ	8"	9169	1995	Current	$9		
2.	Michelline	TJ	7.5"	91815	1996	Current	$13		
3.	Sara II	TJ	6"	91401	1996	Current	$13		
4.	Eleanor	AS	10.5"	5737-01	1995	Current	$14		
5.	Sara	TJ	7.5"	9140	1994	Ret. 1996	N/E		
6.	Josephine	TJ	6"	91701	1996	Current	$9		
7.	Hedy	TJ	10.5"	9186-01	1994	Current	$20		
8.	Jane	AS	10.5"	5737-05	1994	Current	$14		
9.	Mary	AS	10.5"	5737	Pre-92	Current	$14		
10.	Kathryn	AS	7.5"	5732-01	1994	Current	$7		
11.	Camilla	AS	7.5"	5732	1993	Current	$7		
12.	Beecher B. Bunny	JB	10"	5250-10	1996	Current	$16		
13.	Elsinore	AS	7.5"	5732-05	1996	Current	$7		
14.	Diana	AS	10.5"	5738	Pre-92	Current	$14		
15.	Auntie Babbit	TJ	12"	91660	1996	Current	$30		
16.	Veronica	TJ	10.5"	9181	1993	Current	$20		
17.	Peapod	TJ	7.5"	91071	1996	Current	$12		
18.	Anne	AS	7.5"	5734	Pre-92	Current	$7		
19.	Alice	AS	7.5"	5750	1992	Current	$7		
20.	Victoria	AS	7.5"	5736	Pre-92	Current	$7		
21.	Elizabeth	AS	7.5"	5733	Pre-92	Current	$7		

✏️ **PENCIL TOTALS**

Price Paid	Market Value

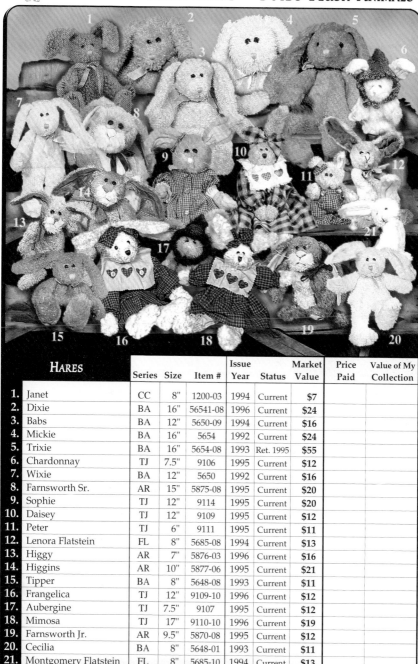

HARES		Series	Size	Item #	Issue Year	Status	Market Value	Price Paid	Value of My Collection
1.	Janet	CC	8"	1200-03	1994	Current	$7		
2.	Dixie	BA	16"	56541-08	1996	Current	$24		
3.	Babs	BA	12"	5650-09	1994	Current	$16		
4.	Mickie	BA	16"	5654	1992	Current	$24		
5.	Trixie	BA	16"	5654-08	1993	Ret. 1995	$55		
6.	Chardonnay	TJ	7.5"	9106	1995	Current	$12		
7.	Wixie	BA	12"	5650	1992	Current	$16		
8.	Farnsworth Sr.	AR	15"	5875-08	1995	Current	$20		
9.	Sophie	TJ	12"	9114	1995	Current	$20		
10.	Daisey	TJ	12"	9109	1995	Current	$12		
11.	Peter	TJ	6"	9111	1995	Current	$11		
12.	Lenora Flatstein	FL	8"	5685-08	1994	Current	$13		
13.	Higgy	AR	7"	5876-03	1996	Current	$16		
14.	Higgins	AR	10"	5877-06	1995	Current	$21		
15.	Tipper	BA	8"	5648-08	1993	Current	$11		
16.	Frangelica	TJ	12"	9109-10	1996	Current	$12		
17.	Aubergine	TJ	7.5"	9107	1995	Current	$12		
18.	Mimosa	TJ	17"	9110-10	1996	Current	$19		
19.	Farnsworth Jr.	AR	9.5"	5870-08	1995	Current	$12		
20.	Cecilia	BA	8"	5648-01	1993	Current	$11		
21.	Montgomery Flatstein	FL	8"	5685-10	1994	Current	$13		
NP	Edina Flatstein	FL	8"	5685-05	1996	Current	$13		

✏ PENCIL TOTALS

PRICE PAID	MARKET VALUE

HARES

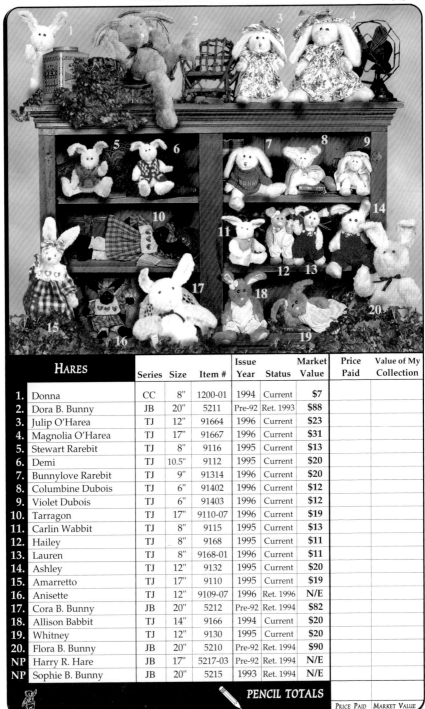

HARES		Series	Size	Item #	Issue Year	Status	Market Value	Price Paid	Value of My Collection
1.	Donna	CC	8"	1200-01	1994	Current	$7		
2.	Dora B. Bunny	JB	20"	5211	Pre-92	Ret. 1993	$88		
3.	Julip O'Harea	TJ	12"	91664	1996	Current	$23		
4.	Magnolia O'Harea	TJ	17"	91667	1996	Current	$31		
5.	Stewart Rarebit	TJ	8"	9116	1995	Current	$13		
6.	Demi	TJ	10.5"	9112	1995	Current	$20		
7.	Bunnylove Rarebit	TJ	9"	91314	1996	Current	$20		
8.	Columbine Dubois	TJ	6"	91402	1996	Current	$12		
9.	Violet Dubois	TJ	6"	91403	1996	Current	$12		
10.	Tarragon	TJ	17"	9110-07	1996	Current	$19		
11.	Carlin Wabbit	TJ	8"	9115	1995	Current	$13		
12.	Hailey	TJ	8"	9168	1995	Current	$11		
13.	Lauren	TJ	8"	9168-01	1996	Current	$11		
14.	Ashley	TJ	12"	9132	1995	Current	$20		
15.	Amarretto	TJ	17"	9110	1995	Current	$19		
16.	Anisette	TJ	17"	9109-07	1996	Ret. 1996	N/E		
17.	Cora B. Bunny	JB	20"	5212	Pre-92	Ret. 1994	$82		
18.	Allison Babbit	TJ	14"	9166	1994	Current	$20		
19.	Whitney	TJ	12"	9130	1995	Current	$20		
20.	Flora B. Bunny	JB	20"	5210	Pre-92	Ret. 1994	$90		
NP	Harry R. Hare	JB	17"	5217-03	Pre-92	Ret. 1994	N/E		
NP	Sophie B. Bunny	JB	20"	5215	1993	Ret. 1994	N/E		

PENCIL TOTALS

PRICE PAID	MARKET VALUE

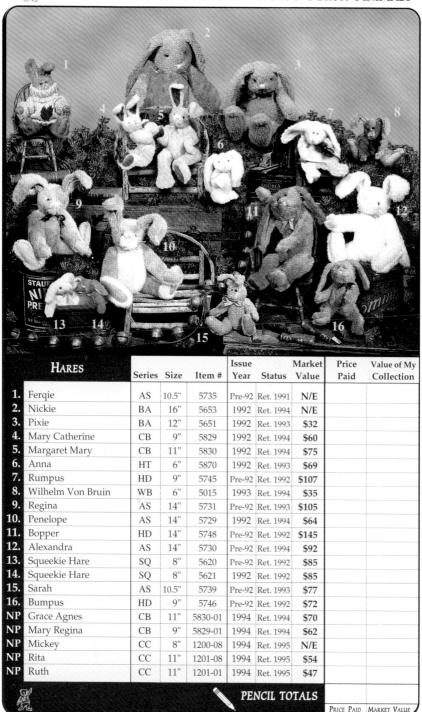

HARES		Series	Size	Item #	Issue Year	Status	Market Value	Price Paid	Value of My Collection
1.	Ferqie	AS	10.5"	5735	Pre-92	Ret. 1991	**N/E**		
2.	Nickie	BA	16"	5653	1992	Ret. 1994	**N/E**		
3.	Pixie	BA	12"	5651	1992	Ret. 1993	**$32**		
4.	Mary Catherine	CB	9"	5829	1992	Ret. 1994	**$60**		
5.	Margaret Mary	CB	11"	5830	1992	Ret. 1994	**$75**		
6.	Anna	HT	6"	5870	1992	Ret. 1993	**$69**		
7.	Rumpus	HD	9"	5745	Pre-92	Ret. 1992	**$107**		
8.	Wilhelm Von Bruin	WB	6"	5015	1993	Ret. 1994	**$35**		
9.	Regina	AS	14"	5731	Pre-92	Ret. 1993	**$105**		
10.	Penelope	AS	14"	5729	1992	Ret. 1994	**$64**		
11.	Bopper	HD	14"	5748	Pre-92	Ret. 1992	**$145**		
12.	Alexandra	AS	14"	5730	Pre-92	Ret. 1994	**$92**		
13.	Squeekie Hare	SQ	8"	5620	Pre-92	Ret. 1992	**$85**		
14.	Squeekie Hare	SQ	8"	5621	1992	Ret. 1992	**$85**		
15.	Sarah	AS	10.5"	5739	Pre-92	Ret. 1993	**$77**		
16.	Bumpus	HD	9"	5746	Pre-92	Ret. 1992	**$72**		
NP	Grace Agnes	CB	11"	5830-01	1994	Ret. 1994	**$70**		
NP	Mary Regina	CB	9"	5829-01	1994	Ret. 1994	**$62**		
NP	Mickey	CC	8"	1200-08	1994	Ret. 1995	**N/E**		
NP	Rita	CC	11"	1201-08	1994	Ret. 1995	**$54**		
NP	Ruth	CC	11"	1201-01	1994	Ret. 1995	**$47**		
	PENCIL TOTALS								
								PRICE PAID	MARKET VALUE

HARES

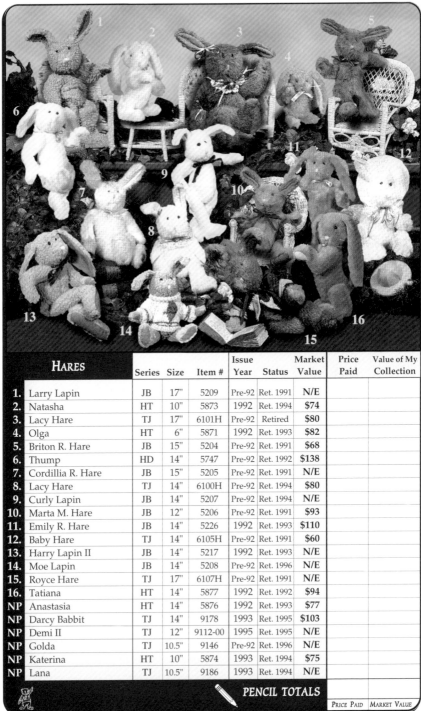

HARES	Series	Size	Item #	Issue Year	Status	Market Value	Price Paid	Value of My Collection
1. Larry Lapin	JB	17"	5209	Pre-92	Ret. 1991	N/E		
2. Natasha	HT	10"	5873	1992	Ret. 1994	$74		
3. Lacy Hare	TJ	17"	6101H	Pre-92	Retired	$80		
4. Olga	HT	6"	5871	1992	Ret. 1993	$82		
5. Briton R. Hare	JB	15"	5204	Pre-92	Ret. 1991	$68		
6. Thump	HD	14"	5747	Pre-92	Ret. 1992	$138		
7. Cordillia R. Hare	JB	15"	5205	Pre-92	Ret. 1991	N/E		
8. Lacy Hare	TJ	14"	6100H	Pre-92	Ret. 1994	$80		
9. Curly Lapin	JB	14"	5207	Pre-92	Ret. 1994	N/E		
10. Marta M. Hare	JB	12"	5206	Pre-92	Ret. 1991	$93		
11. Emily R. Hare	JB	14"	5226	1992	Ret. 1993	$110		
12. Baby Hare	TJ	14"	6105H	Pre-92	Ret. 1991	$60		
13. Harry Lapin II	JB	14"	5217	1992	Ret. 1993	N/E		
14. Moe Lapin	JB	14"	5208	Pre-92	Ret. 1996	N/E		
15. Royce Hare	TJ	17"	6107H	Pre-92	Ret. 1991	N/E		
16. Tatiana	HT	14"	5877	1992	Ret. 1992	$94		
NP Anastasia	HT	14"	5876	1992	Ret. 1993	$77		
NP Darcy Babbit	TJ	14"	9178	1993	Ret. 1995	$103		
NP Demi II	TJ	12"	9112-00	1995	Ret. 1995	N/E		
NP Golda	TJ	10.5"	9146	Pre-92	Ret. 1996	N/E		
NP Katerina	HT	10"	5874	1993	Ret. 1994	$75		
NP Lana	TJ	10.5"	9186	1993	Ret. 1994	N/E		
					PENCIL TOTALS			
							PRICE PAID	MARKET VALUE

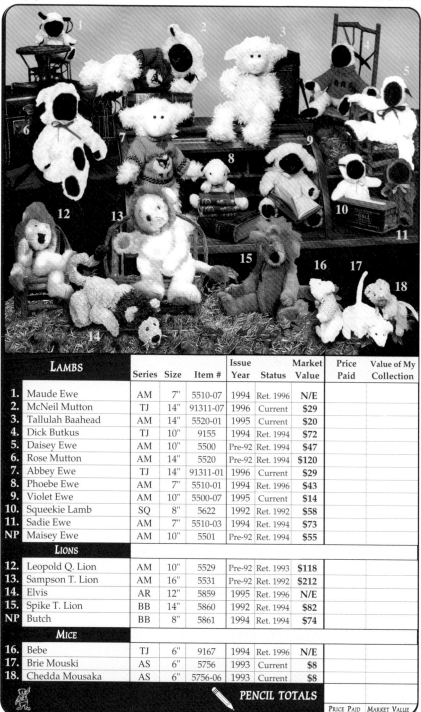

	LAMBS	Series	Size	Item #	Issue Year	Status	Market Value	Price Paid	Value of My Collection
1.	Maude Ewe	AM	7"	5510-07	1994	Ret. 1996	N/E		
2.	McNeil Mutton	TJ	14"	91311-07	1996	Current	$29		
3.	Tallulah Baahead	AM	14"	5520-01	1995	Current	$20		
4.	Dick Butkus	TJ	10"	9155	1994	Ret. 1994	$72		
5.	Daisey Ewe	AM	10"	5500	Pre-92	Ret. 1994	$47		
6.	Rose Mutton	AM	14"	5520	Pre-92	Ret. 1994	$120		
7.	Abbey Ewe	TJ	14"	91311-01	1996	Current	$29		
8.	Phoebe Ewe	AM	7"	5510-01	1994	Ret. 1996	$43		
9.	Violet Ewe	AM	10"	5500-07	1995	Current	$14		
10.	Squeekie Lamb	SQ	8"	5622	1992	Ret. 1992	$58		
11.	Sadie Ewe	AM	7"	5510-03	1994	Ret. 1994	$73		
NP	Maisey Ewe	AM	10"	5501	Pre-92	Ret. 1994	$55		
	LIONS								
12.	Leopold Q. Lion	AM	10"	5529	Pre-92	Ret. 1993	$118		
13.	Sampson T. Lion	AM	16"	5531	Pre-92	Ret. 1992	$212		
14.	Elvis	AR	12"	5859	1995	Ret. 1996	N/E		
15.	Spike T. Lion	BB	14"	5860	1992	Ret. 1994	$82		
NP	Butch	BB	8"	5861	1994	Ret. 1994	$74		
	MICE								
16.	Bebe	TJ	6"	9167	1994	Ret. 1996	N/E		
17.	Brie Mouski	AS	6"	5756	1993	Current	$8		
18.	Chedda Mousaka	AS	6"	5756-06	1993	Current	$8		
						PENCIL TOTALS			
								PRICE PAID	MARKET VALUE

LAMBS/LIONS/MICE

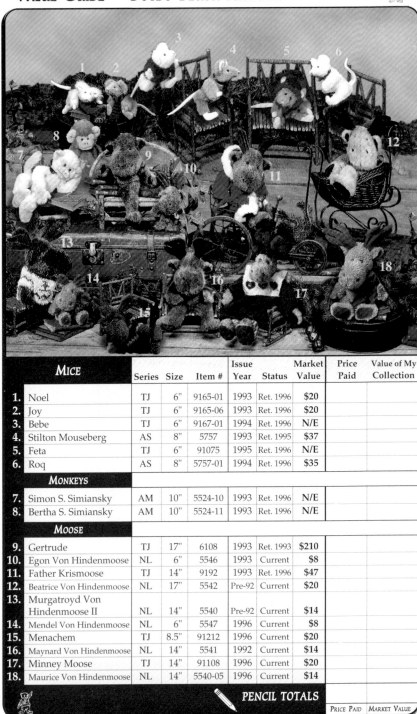

MICE	Series	Size	Item #	Issue Year	Status	Market Value	Price Paid	Value of My Collection
1. Noel	TJ	6"	9165-01	1993	Ret. 1996	$20		
2. Joy	TJ	6"	9165-06	1993	Ret. 1996	$20		
3. Bebe	TJ	6"	9167-01	1994	Ret. 1996	N/E		
4. Stilton Mouseberg	AS	8"	5757	1993	Ret. 1995	$37		
5. Feta	TJ	6"	91075	1995	Ret. 1996	N/E		
6. Roq	AS	8"	5757-01	1994	Ret. 1996	$35		
MONKEYS								
7. Simon S. Simiansky	AM	10"	5524-10	1993	Ret. 1996	N/E		
8. Bertha S. Simiansky	AM	10"	5524-11	1993	Ret. 1996	N/E		
MOOSE								
9. Gertrude	TJ	17"	6108	1993	Ret. 1993	$210		
10. Egon Von Hindenmoose	NL	6"	5546	1993	Current	$8		
11. Father Krismoose	TJ	14"	9192	1993	Ret. 1996	$47		
12. Beatrice Von Hindenmoose	NL	17"	5542	Pre-92	Current	$20		
13. Murgatroyd Von Hindenmoose II	NL	14"	5540	Pre-92	Current	$14		
14. Mendel Von Hindenmoose	NL	6"	5547	1996	Current	$8		
15. Menachem	TJ	8.5"	91212	1996	Current	$20		
16. Maynard Von Hindenmoose	NL	14"	5541	1992	Current	$14		
17. Minney Moose	TJ	14"	91108	1996	Current	$20		
18. Maurice Von Hindenmoose	NL	14"	5540-05	1996	Current	$14		
					PENCIL TOTALS		Price Paid	Market Value

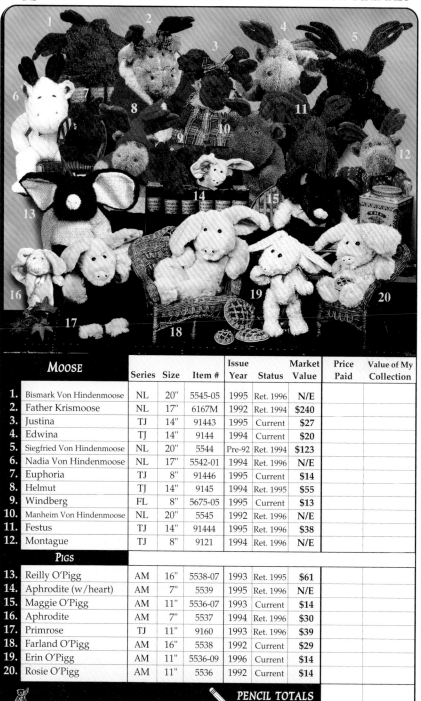

	MOOSE	Series	Size	Item #	Issue Year	Status	Market Value	Price Paid	Value of My Collection
1.	Bismark Von Hindenmoose	NL	20"	5545-05	1995	Ret. 1996	N/E		
2.	Father Krismoose	NL	17"	6167M	1992	Ret. 1994	$240		
3.	Justina	TJ	14"	91443	1995	Current	$27		
4.	Edwina	TJ	14"	9144	1994	Current	$20		
5.	Siegfried Von Hindenmoose	NL	20"	5544	Pre-92	Ret. 1994	$123		
6.	Nadia Von Hindenmoose	NL	17"	5542-01	1994	Ret. 1996	N/E		
7.	Euphoria	TJ	8"	91446	1995	Current	$14		
8.	Helmut	TJ	14"	9145	1994	Ret. 1995	$55		
9.	Windberg	FL	8"	5675-05	1995	Current	$13		
10.	Manheim Von Hindenmoose	NL	20"	5545	1992	Ret. 1996	N/E		
11.	Festus	TJ	14"	91444	1995	Ret. 1996	$38		
12.	Montague	TJ	8"	9121	1994	Ret. 1996	N/E		
	PIGS								
13.	Reilly O'Pigg	AM	16"	5538-07	1993	Ret. 1995	$61		
14.	Aphrodite (w/heart)	AM	7"	5539	1995	Ret. 1996	N/E		
15.	Maggie O'Pigg	AM	11"	5536-07	1993	Current	$14		
16.	Aphrodite	AM	7"	5537	1994	Ret. 1996	$30		
17.	Primrose	TJ	11"	9160	1993	Ret. 1996	$39		
18.	Farland O'Pigg	AM	16"	5538	1992	Current	$29		
19.	Erin O'Pigg	AM	11"	5536-09	1996	Current	$14		
20.	Rosie O'Pigg	AM	11"	5536	1992	Current	$14		

PENCIL TOTALS

PRICE PAID	MARKET VALUE

MOOSE/PIGS

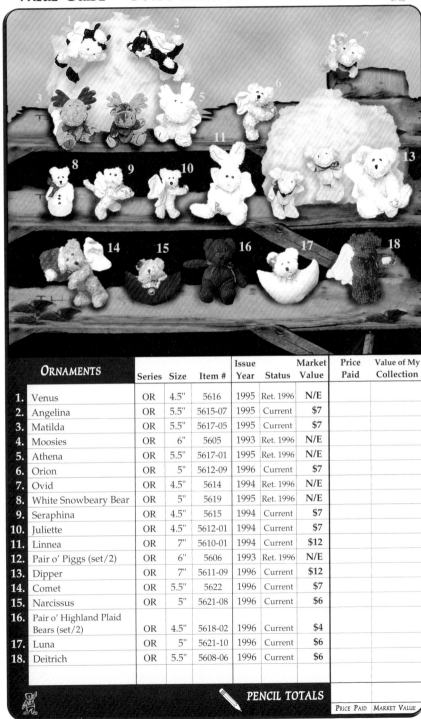

ORNAMENTS		Series	Size	Item #	Issue Year	Status	Market Value	Price Paid	Value of My Collection
1.	Venus	OR	4.5"	5616	1995	Ret. 1996	N/E		
2.	Angelina	OR	5.5"	5615-07	1995	Current	$7		
3.	Matilda	OR	5.5"	5617-05	1995	Current	$7		
4.	Moosies	OR	6"	5605	1993	Ret. 1996	N/E		
5.	Athena	OR	5.5"	5617-01	1995	Ret. 1996	N/E		
6.	Orion	OR	5"	5612-09	1996	Current	$7		
7.	Ovid	OR	4.5"	5614	1994	Ret. 1996	N/E		
8.	White Snowbeary Bear	OR	5"	5619	1995	Ret. 1996	N/E		
9.	Seraphina	OR	4.5"	5615	1994	Current	$7		
10.	Juliette	OR	4.5"	5612-01	1994	Current	$7		
11.	Linnea	OR	7"	5610-01	1994	Current	$12		
12.	Pair o' Piggs (set/2)	OR	6"	5606	1993	Ret. 1996	N/E		
13.	Dipper	OR	7"	5611-09	1996	Current	$12		
14.	Comet	OR	5.5"	5622	1996	Current	$7		
15.	Narcissus	OR	5"	5621-08	1996	Current	$6		
16.	Pair o' Highland Plaid Bears (set/2)	OR	4.5"	5618-02	1996	Current	$4		
17.	Luna	OR	5"	5621-10	1996	Current	$6		
18.	Deitrich	OR	5.5"	5608-06	1996	Current	$6		
						PENCIL TOTALS		Price Paid	Market Value

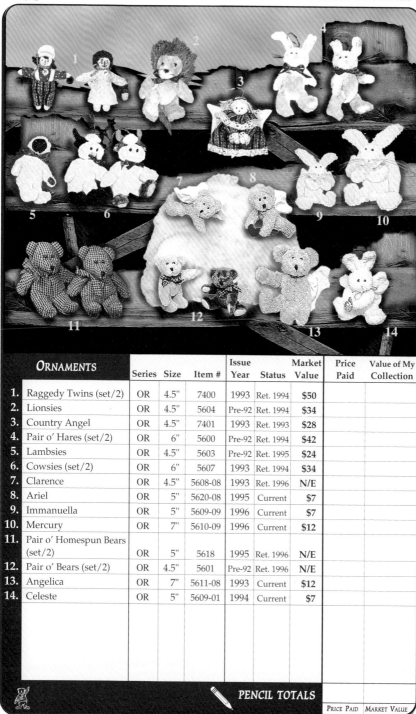

	ORNAMENTS	Series	Size	Item #	Issue Year	Status	Market Value	Price Paid	Value of My Collection
1.	Raggedy Twins (set/2)	OR	4.5"	7400	1993	Ret. 1994	**$50**		
2.	Lionsies	OR	4.5"	5604	Pre-92	Ret. 1994	**$34**		
3.	Country Angel	OR	4.5"	7401	1993	Ret. 1993	**$28**		
4.	Pair o' Hares (set/2)	OR	6"	5600	Pre-92	Ret. 1994	**$42**		
5.	Lambsies	OR	4.5"	5603	Pre-92	Ret. 1995	**$24**		
6.	Cowsies (set/2)	OR	6"	5607	1993	Ret. 1994	**$34**		
7.	Clarence	OR	4.5"	5608-08	1993	Ret. 1996	**N/E**		
8.	Ariel	OR	5"	5620-08	1995	Current	**$7**		
9.	Immanuella	OR	5"	5609-09	1996	Current	**$7**		
10.	Mercury	OR	7"	5610-09	1996	Current	**$12**		
11.	Pair o' Homespun Bears (set/2)	OR	5"	5618	1995	Ret. 1996	**N/E**		
12.	Pair o' Bears (set/2)	OR	4.5"	5601	Pre-92	Ret. 1996	**N/E**		
13.	Angelica	OR	7"	5611-08	1993	Current	**$12**		
14.	Celeste	OR	5"	5609-01	1994	Current	**$7**		
			PENCIL TOTALS					PRICE PAID	MARKET VALUE

Value Guide — Boyds Plush Animals

Use these pages to record future Boyds Plush releases.

Future Releases	Series	Size	Item #	Issue Year	Status	Market Value	Price Paid	Value of My Collection

PENCIL TOTALS

Price Paid	Market Value

FUTURE RELEASES	Series	Size	Item #	Issue Year	Status	Market Value	Price Paid	Value of My Collection
							PENCIL TOTALS	
							Price Paid	Market Value

Total Value Of My Collection

Record the value of your collection here by adding the pencil totals from the bottom of each value guide page.

BOYDS PLUSH ANIMALS	Price Paid	Market Value
Page 87		
Page 88		
Page 89		
Page 90		
Page 91		
Page 92		
Page 93		
Page 94		
Page 95		
Page 96		
Page 97		
Page 98		
Page 99		
Page 100		
Page 101		
Page 102		
Page 103		
TOTAL		

BOYDS PLUSH ANIMALS	Price Paid	Market Value
Page 104		
Page 105		
Page 106		
Page 107		
Page 108		
Page 109		
Page 110		
Page 111		
Page 112		
Page 113		
Page 114		
Page 115		
Page 116		
Page 117		
Page 118		
Page 119		
Page 120		
Page 121		
TOTAL		

GRAND TOTALS	PRICE PAID	MARKET VALUE

COLLECTOR'S
VALUE GUIDE™

Plush Exclusives

Among the astounding number of plush animals produced by The Boyds Collection Ltd. over the years are several that have been highly limited or offered exclusively through selected outlets. Because of their limited quantities, these plush animals are extremely difficult for even the most devoted collectors to find. Many of these plush animals were offered through QVC, and as The Boyds Collection Ltd. maintains an increasingly strong presence on the home shopping program, collectors can anticipate more exclusives in the future. There also have been exclusive Boyds plush musicals issued by the San Francisco Music Box Company.

Background information on these special releases is sketchy. The name and edition size, if known, are provided along with a box allowing you to check the plush animals you have in your collection. Because we want this publication to be as accurate as possible for Boyds collectors, we encourage you to contact us if you know of any plush animals (both older plush in the general collection as well as exclusives) that we have overlooked. Any information we receive will be researched before it is published as "fact."

COLLECTORS' PUBLISHING CO., INC.

Attn: Boyds Bearfinder

598 Pomeroy Avenue

Meriden, CT 06450

http://www.collectorspub.com

	Edition Size			Edition Size
❏ Aletha The Bearmaker	500		❏ Hedda	2400
❏ Angel Ornaments (set/3)	----		❏ Holly	----
❏ Ashley (musical)	----		❏ Lapis (ornament)	----
❏ Auntie Adina	500		❏ Memsy	400
❏ Betty Lou	----		❏ Molly	400
❏ Busby Bear	----		❏ Mrs. Bearburg	
❏ Caroline	----		(w/basket & bears)	----
❏ Christmas Bears (set/3)	----		❏ Mrs. Fiedler (w/instrument)	500
❏ Clara	3600		❏ Mrs. Hortense	250
❏ Delaney And The Duffer	500		❏ Ms. Odetta (w/student &	
❏ Duffer The Golfer On Bench	500		chalkboard)	1200
❏ Eddie Bauer Edmund	----		❏ Nettie	300
❏ Emma R. Hare			❏ Pansy (w/2 bears)	1200
(Grandma Babbit)	1200		❏ Pauline	3600
❏ Eugenia (musical)	----		❏ Smith Witter II (musical)	----
❏ Father Chrisbear & Son	750		❏ Teddy Bauer (w/exclusive	
❏ Father Christmoose	400		sweater)	----
❏ Hattie & Annie	150		❏ Witch-Ma-Call-It & Spook	500

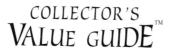

COLLECTOR'S

VALUE GUIDE™

Secondary Market Overview

Most people collect Boyds Bears for a very simple reason – they love 'em! They love the poseability of the plush animals and the artistic quality of the resin figurines, all of which are available at very affordable prices. Only recently have some collectors begun to look at their Boyds collection as a possible "collectible" investment and this is where the secondary market comes in.

For most collectible lines, secondary market demand is created when pieces are removed from production and are no longer available in retail stores. This results in an increase in their value, based on collector demand for these now hard-to-find pieces. Frequently, there is a range of prices on each piece and not one hard and fast dollar value. Secondary market prices can fluctuate, even from day to day; it all depends on what price collectors are selling their pieces for and, more importantly, whether other collectors are willing to pay that price.

1. How does the Boyds secondary market work?

A. Retired Pieces

As with most collectible lines, the Boyds Bears secondary market begins when a piece is retired and is no longer available from retailers. Once dealer stock of these pieces is depleted, collectors have to look elsewhere to find them, most commonly from other collectors. Because retired pieces are no longer produced by the company, demand quickly surpasses the available supply; consequently, retired pieces increase in value, sometimes as much as double or triple the original retail price. As The Boyds Collection Ltd. retires more and more pieces, this traditional secondary market demand will grow accordingly.

There are a few retired Bearstone figurines that, because of their scarcity, have become valuable on the secondary market. "Father Chrisbear And Son" is very difficult to find, as it was one of the first Bearstone pieces produced in June of 1993 and then retired six months later. Only one edition of this piece was produced before it was retired (see explanation of Boyds edition numbers on next page). As a result, those who collect only low edition numbers and those who look for any

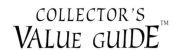

COLLECTOR'S
VALUE GUIDE™

edition they can get their hands on to complete their collections are fighting it out for the same limited number of pieces! The same is true for another piece which was available for six months in 1993, "Grenville . . . With Green Scarf." In 1995, a version of "Bailey The Baker . . . With Sweetie Pie" was available at the Teddy Bear Festival in Clarion, Iowa. This piece, the "Clarion Bear" (#2254CL), was produced in one edition (3,600 pieces), and has become a coveted piece on the secondary market.

With Boyds plush animals, there are no edition numbers, so most of the secondary market activity is on the retired characters. The most coveted Boyds plush animals on the secondary market are the annual limited editions "Bailey," "Edmund" and "Emily." These limited editions are available for one year only in retail stores. The secondary market for Boyds plush animals is a very new (but growing) phenomenon and not all retired characters have seen activity on the secondary market.

B. Editions

For the Boyds resin figurines, The Boyds Collection Ltd. uses "edition" numbers to keep track of how many pieces have been produced. This method of keeping track of how many pieces are produced has resulted in a secondary market demand among some collectors for the earliest editions of each piece.

For the Bearstones and Folkstones, there are 3,600 pieces in each edition, while The Shoe Box Bears have 6,000 pieces per edition. For the Dollstones, 4,800 pieces make up an edition. However, the Boyds Collection Ltd. has indicated that the edition system for the Bearstones may soon change, possibly for the fall 1997 releases. This could mean an increase in the number of pieces in each edition (to 4,800, 9,600 or even higher) or the adoption of new bottomstamp markings to identify when pieces were produced. Whichever way the system is changed, it is bound to affect the Bearstone secondary market; but it's anyone's guess at this point exactly how.

The edition number is marked on the bottom of the piece, along with the piece number in that edition. So, if you turn over your "Homer On

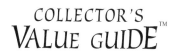

Secondary Market Overview

The Plate" and the number begins with "1E," you know this piece is among the first 3,600 pieces produced. If you see "2E/100," you have the 100th piece in the second edition (or, the 3,700th piece overall). Unless there has been a mold change or a color change from previous editions, there is no significant difference in appearance between a 1E and a 22E piece.

Right now, the majority of the secondary market demand for Boyds pieces is for the 1E pieces. As more collectors vie for the small number of 1E's, demand is on the rise for the next earliest pieces, the 2E's and 3E's. The Dollstone figurines featured on QVC have been marked as "Premier Editions" and although there are also "standard" 1E versions of these figurines, the Premier Editions, at the moment, are considered more valuable by many Dollstone collectors (see *Value Guide* section for pricing). Keep in mind that the edition numbers are only used on the Boyds resin figurines and not the plush animals.

There has been some concern that the edition numbers can be modified by collectors to appear to be lower than they really are (e.g., removing the first digit of "11E," "21E," etc. so that only "1E" is left). While it's doubtful that this is a common practice, the general lesson – always make sure you get what you pay for – is an important one for collectors active on the secondary market.

II. Where is the secondary market?

There are various ways in which collectors can buy and sell pieces on the secondary market. The first step is to check with your retailer, as many retailers act as middlemen or have connections with other collectors. The easiest and most direct way to reach other collectors is through a *secondary market exchange service*. Collectors list the pieces they wish to sell or buy with the exchange service, which publishes a list of the pieces and the asking price. The exchange acts as the middleman in the transaction for a commission on each completed sale (usually between 10% and 20%). There also are exchange services that sell their own pieces and not those of collectors; there would be no commission in

these cases. One benefit of using an exchange service is that you can reach collectors all over the country with minimal work. Most exchange listings are published monthly and may require a subscription or membership fee. A few generate daily listings which collectors can call for and receive by mail. Each piece is typically listed with the price the seller is asking and the edition number on the bottom of the piece (for example, "Clara . . . 'The Nurse,'" 1E, $325; "Bessie The Santa Cow," 3E, $25, etc.). On page 128 is a listing of some secondary market exchange services, secondary market dealers and newsletters that deal with Boyds resin figurines and plush collectibles.

Many newsletters and magazines feature their own "swap & sell" sections, which operate much the same way as the exchange services. Some collectors place *classified advertisements* in their local newspapers (under Antiques/Collectibles), but it may take longer to sell or find pieces this way because newspapers reach a general readership and not collectors specifically.

The newest and perhaps most exciting secondary market source is the *Internet* via home computer. Here, collectors can find a wealth of information on Boyds Bears without leaving their homes! Many of the websites and entries are retail stores that carry Boyds Bears and may be active on the secondary market; or bulletin boards where collectors can trade, buy and sell pieces. The virtue of these on-line price listings is that they can be updated immediately and can be used for quick sales or trades. The best way to get Boyds information on the Internet is to use the search functions. Because information is only loosely organized and there can be thousands of entries, it's best to be as specific as possible. You may want to search for specific essential phrases, such as "Bearstone AND secondary" or "Boyds AND plush AND Bailey." These searches will lead you to retailers, collectors, publishers and secondary market dealers who can help you find what you're looking for.

Some *retailers* are also active on the secondary market, either working as an exchange service or selling directly to collectors. If a collector wants to sell a large number of pieces or an entire collection, contacting a

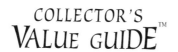

Secondary Market Overview

retailer may be ideal because of the dollar amounts involved. Other retailers who don't buy and sell secondary market pieces may sponsor secondary market collector shows as a service to their customers. Local and regional collector clubs also sponsor secondary market events.

Whether you're buying or selling on the secondary market, an important factor to consider is the packaging of the pieces. In the "real world," a box is just a box; but in the world of collectibles, boxes can actually affect the secondary market value of your pieces. Not only are the boxes perfect for storage and protection of your figurines, but many collectors will consider a piece sold without its original packaging to be "incomplete," and these pieces will generally command a lower price on the secondary market.

EXCHANGES, DEALERS AND NEWSLETTERS

Boyds Bear Retail Inquirer
P.O. Box 4385
Gettysburg, PA 17325
(general Boyds information written by the Head Bean Hisself; check your local store for copies!)

Bear Tales & Trails
Harry Croft
518 N. Everett Drive
Palatine, IL 60067-4110
(847) 358-6276

Collectible Exchange, Inc.
6621 Columbiana Road
New Middletown, OH 44442
(216) 542-9646

Donna's Collector's Choice Exchange
163 Longleaf Pine Circle
Sanford, FL 32773
1-800-480-5105

Ed & Janet Hymes
487 E. Independence
Jacksonville, IL 62650
(217) 245-4603

New England Collectibles Exchange
Bob Dorman
201 Pine Avenue
Clarksburg, MA 01247
1-800-854-6323

Roger's Collectors' Marketplace
Roger Poole
8017 N. Hughes Drive
Spokane, WA 99208
(509) 467-2300

Mary Jo Truax
P.O. Box 273
101 So. First Street
Ridgeview, SD 57652

COLLECTOR'S
VALUE GUIDE™

Variations

Sharp-eyed collectors who compare two of the same Boyds resin pieces may find slight differences, such as the size of a flower, the color of a hat or the number of buttons on a dress. Some of these variations result because the pieces are handmade and handpainted; but some variations, especially the more important changes that might affect the secondary market value of a piece, come as the result of changes to the production molds. Listed here are some of the variations that we've uncovered with the help of experienced Boyds collectors, particularly Harry Croft, publisher of the *Bear Tales & Trails* newsletter.

BEARSTONE VARIATIONS

Bailey Bear With Suitcase (#2000)

This piece, which normally has rough-textured fur and a white underside, has been found with smooth fur and a brown underside. There are thought to be about 11,000 pieces with this variation, but they are all marked as 1E.

Standard Version   *Variation*

Bailey ... In The Orchard (#2006)

Originally, the paw print on this piece appeared on the cider jug, but it has since been moved to appear on Bailey's dress. The change seems to have occurred around the 22nd edition.

Bailey The Baker ... With Sweetie Pie (#2254)

A variation of this piece, known as the "Clarion Bear," was available at the Teddy Bear Festival in Clarion, Iowa, in June 1995 (only 3,600 pieces were produced). "Clarion, Iowa" is printed on the pie and Bailey wears a pink bow.

Standard Version   *Variation*

Byron & Chedda With Catmint (#2010)

Until the third edition or so, Byron had no patches on his left arm and no stitches on his hat.

Variations

Edmund The Elf Bear . . .
Holiday Glow (#2772, votive)

The imprint on the bottom, "It Was The Night Before Christmas," was misspelled on some pieces to read "I Was The Night Before Christmas."

Elliot . . . The Hero (#2280)

The word "Bearstone" is misspelled on the bottom of some pieces to read "Beatstone."

Grenville & Beatrice . . .
Best Friends (#2016)

This piece has been found with the dove positioned on the right side of the stone base instead of front and center.

Standard Version   *Variation*

Grenville & Neville . . . The Sign (#2099)

The underside of this piece has been brown as well as the standard white.

Moriarty – The Bear In
The Cat Suit (#2005)

The copyright year ("1993") appears on the side of the base in early editions, as opposed to the top of the base. Also, Moriarty's hood and cuffs are smaller than in recent editions.

Ms. Griz . . . Monday
Morning (#2276)

The first six editions of this figurine feature Ms. Griz in a pink dress, while in later editions her dress is blue-green.

Standard Version   *Variation*

Simone de Bearvoire & Her Mom, My Auntie Alice (#2001)

Early editions are much less detailed and are missing the patches on "mom's" paws.

Standard Version   *Variation*

SAN FRANCISCO MUSIC BOX VARIATIONS

Boyds Arthur On Trunk (#2751)
This music box has been found with a larger trunk and thicker tassels on the scarf covering the trunk.

Boyds Ted & Teddy (#2701)
Early versions of this piece are slightly larger than later ones.

Boyds Wilson With Love Sonnets (#2750)
In early versions, the bottom book is larger, the song was "You're Nobody 'Til Somebody Loves You" and the bear and books were made from one mold.

FOLKSTONE VARIATIONS

Beatrice . . . The Birthday Angel (#2825)
Variations of this piece include obscure writing on the bow and a taller "Beatrice."

Betty Biscuit (#2870)
Early editions can be found with the original title, "Betty Cocker."

Florence . . . The Kitchen Angel (#2824)
Before there was a mold change to this piece, "Florence" could be found with a longer skirt and with her hand on the bottom center of the bowl.

Lizzie . . . The Shopping Angel (#2827)
Variations include Lizzie's right hand on the purse strap and many folds in the bottom of her skirt.

Minerva . . . The Baseball Angel (#2826)
In some figurines, six buttons appear on her jersey instead of seven.

DOLLSTONE VARIATIONS

Jean With Elliot & Debbie . . . The Bakers (#3510)
A special version of this figurine was produced under item #3510-01 in which Jean's dress and ribbon are red instead of purple and green, respectively.

Standard Version *Variation*

PLUSH VARIATIONS

Bailey (#9199-05, Spring 1996, bear)
Most collectors will recognize Bailey's dress from Spring 1996 as being velveteen, but 4,800 of these Baileys were made exclusively for QVC with "shiny purple" dresses.

Edmund (#9175-01, Spring 1994, bear)
Originally produced with a navy and cream checkered shirt, Edmund also appeared in a black-and-white checkered shirt.

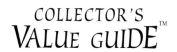

COLLECTOR'S
VALUE GUIDE™

Variations

OTHER VARIATIONS

Some Folkstone and Bearstone figurines are marked as "GRS" or "RS" editions. This notation identifies pieces that have been made from a mold that has been "resculpted." These editions usually begin at 1E, regardless of how many editions were produced before the mold was changed. Therefore, these pieces would typically have regular 1E's *and* GRS 1E's. There are various reasons why a mold might be resculpted. It could be because of structural problems with a piece – for example, if part of the piece is fragile and keeps breaking off. Eventually, the production molds break with so much wear and tear, and sometimes the molds will be changed when they're recast.

The Boyds Collection Ltd. has also produced exclusive figurines for Boyds Bears retailers in Canada. These pieces, which are available only "over the border," have become a popular find on the secondary market here in the United States. There have been six Canadian Bearstone figurines, including two based on U.S. pieces; a Canadian Folkstone piece; and a Canadian Dollstone figurine based on the U.S. piece, "Betsey With Edmund . . . The Patriots."

Increasingly, The Boyds Collection Ltd. has produced exclusive pieces (including special recolored versions) that have been available only through select retailers. Because of their highly limited quantities, these pieces tend to come and go before many collectors even know of their existence.

Another category of exclusive pieces are those that are produced for QVC, the home shopping channel. Not only have there been plush bears that were available only through QVC, but many Dollstone pieces have debuted on QVC before becoming available in retail stores. These QVC Dollstone pieces are marked as "Premier Editions" and are considered unique and particularly valuable among Dollstone collectors (see *Value Guide* section for pricing).

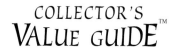

COLLECTOR'S
VALUE GUIDE™

Insuring Your Collection

While the pieces in your collection hold sentimental value, they also have a dollar value. When you add up each purchase, you may find that you've invested quite a bit putting your collection together. Then, when you look at the secondary market values and figure out what it would cost to replace pieces in your collection, you might decide you want to insure your collection just as you insure the other valuables in your home. There are three steps to determining whether you should insure your collection: *knowing your current coverage, documenting the contents and value of your collection* and *weighing the risk.*

1. Know your coverage

Collectibles are considered part of the contents of a house and as such, they are typically included in homeowners or renters insurance policies. Ask your agent about the types of loss or damage your policy covers and what it doesn't cover. A standard policy covers household contents for damage or loss from perils such as fire, hurricanes and theft. Common exclusions include earthquakes, floods and breakage through routine handling. In addition to determining the types of loss that are covered, ask your agent about the dollar value that would be paid out in the event that you have to file a claim. The amount paid out will vary based on the type of coverage you have. Today, most insurance policies are written at replacement value which would provide enough money to replace a lost or damaged collection. Replacement value policies pay out the amount needed to actually replace the items which is especially important for collectibles because they appreciate in value.

2. Document the contents and value of your collection

In order to determine how much coverage you need, you must first document your collection to calculate how much it would cost to replace your pieces. There are many ways to document your collection, from a simple listing to hiring an appraiser, but you should check with your insurance agent first to find out what records the insurance company will accept in the event of a loss. Generally companies want to see proof that you own particular pieces and proof of their value.

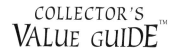
COLLECTOR'S
VALUE GUIDE™

Insuring Your Collection

Two of the best forms of documentation are receipts and a "schedule" or listing of each piece in your collection, including the purchase date, price paid, where you purchased the piece, special markings and secondary market value. Some companies will accept a reputable secondary market guide such as the Collector's Value Guide for pricing.

Two features of the Collector's Value Guide are designed to aid you if you decide to insure your collection. The *Value Guide* section includes 1997 secondary market prices to help you determine the replacement value of your pieces. Keep in mind that your insurance carrier may want to distinguish between items which are available through normal retail outlets versus pieces which are no longer available (i.e., retired). Because of the unique nature of the Boyds secondary market, a resource like the Collector's Value Guide is important in showing that a 1E piece may have a higher secondary market value even though the same piece with a different edition number is still available in retail stores. It makes sense to list or "schedule" your valuable pieces on your policy, just as you would for jewelry and other important valuables.

To ensure proper coverage, it is important that your agent understands secondary market values. If you have particularly valuable pieces or if you have an extensive collection, you should note that the more valuable the item, the more demanding the insurance company will be for industry-accepted valuation. In some cases, the carrier may even want a professional appraisal. For appraisers in your area, contact the American Society of Appraisers at 1-800-ASA-VALU.

Photographs and video footage of your Boyds pieces are a good back-up in case of an unforeseen problem claim. Snapshots and video should record closeup views of the piece. With your Boyds collection, it's especially important to photograph the bottoms of your pieces where the edition numbers are found. Print two sets of photographs; store one set in your home and give the second set to a friend or put it in a safe deposit box.

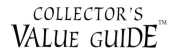

COLLECTOR'S
VALUE GUIDE™

3. Weigh the risk

After you calculate the replacement cost of your collection, you can determine if you have adequate insurance to cover any losses. To do this, add the estimated value of your home furnishings to the value of your collectibles (as totaled in this book) and consult your insurance policy for the amount of coverage. Compare the total value of the contents of your home to the dollar amount you would be paid in the event that you had to file a claim.

If you find your policy does not provide enough coverage, you could purchase additional insurance for your collectibles. This can be done by adding a "Personal Articles Floater" (PAF) or a "Fine Arts Floater" or "rider" to your homeowners policy which provides broader coverage and insures your collection for specific dollar amounts. Another option is to purchase a separate policy specifically for collectibles from a specialized insurance provider. One such company is American Collectors Insurance, Inc. in Cherry Hill, New Jersey, which offers coverage for a wide variety of collectibles, from figurines to dolls to memorabilia. A sample application form is shown here. You can reach American Collectors Insurance at: 1-800-257-5758.

Apply Now For A Collectibles Insurance Policy
COLLECTIBLES INSURANCE POLICY APPLICATION
Underwritten by American Bankers Insurance Company of Florida

sample application

As with all insurance, you must weigh the risk of loss against the cost of additional coverage.

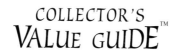

Collectors' Corner

The Boyds Collection Ltd. Biography

The Boyds Collection Ltd. story begins with chief designer, president and the "Head Bean," Gary Lowenthal. Born and raised in New York City, Lowenthal left his home to attend Alfred University in Upstate New York where he received a B.S. and an M.S. in Biology. With degree in hand, he headed towards the Fiji Islands with the U.S. Peace Corps and then returned to his own native island of Manhattan. There he entered the highly fashionable world of Bloomingdales and served a seven year stint in the purchasing, design and merchandising department (that's where those ever-so-dapper *T.J.'s Best Dressed* get their fashion sense).

In 1979, Lowenthal left the Big Apple once again in search of greener pastures in Boyds, Maryland, where he opened up an antique shop called The Boyds Collection Ltd. There he made his debut in the world of collectibles with a line of wooden duck decoys, which he followed up with the introduction of a series of miniature ceramic houses called The Gnomes Homes. In 1987, Gary Lowenthal packed up his operations and brought them to Gettysburg, Pennsylvania where, with the help of teddy bear designer Gae Sharp, he began producing a line of plush teddy bears, rabbits and moose (as well as an assortment of other critters).

In 1993, based on the success of his plush line, Gary Lowenthal introduced The Bearstone Collection, a line of sculpted resin figurines based on the lovable characters in the plush line. The popularity of the Bearstones gave rise to more resin collections: The Folkstone Collection (1994), The Dollstone Collection (1996) and The Shoe Box Bears (1996).

Recently, Gary Lowenthal discovered the benefits that the world of technology has to offer the world of collectibles as he began making appearances on the popular television home shopping network, QVC. With the aid of a few transmitter beams and satellites, Lowenthal and his furry friends were transported into living rooms all over the country of collectors and non-collectors alike. Now with regularly scheduled appearances, the Head Bean has entered a new realm in building a loyal Boyds following.

COLLECTOR'S
VALUE GUIDE™

The quality and popularity of Lowenthal's whimsical creations have not gone unnoticed and many pieces have been nominated for and won numerous awards. Among the winners are the plush "Eddie Beanbauer" and the resin "Ms. Bruin & Bailey . . . The Lesson," recipients of the 1995 *Teddy Bear & Friends Magazine*'s TOBY® Award and the plush, "Wilson," honored with the 1992 *Teddy Bear Review Magazine*'s Golden Teddy Award.

Production, Packaging And Pricing

1. Resin Figurines

The inventive mind behind the creation of the resin figurines is none other than that of Gary Lowenthal, the Head Bean Hisself! Based on sketches created from Lowenthal's ideas, a Master Sculptor carves the image into clay, which will serve as the basis for the production molds. The sculpture then goes through a period of evaluation and once it receives everyone's approval, it is cast into a "White Ware" casting original. Next, the original is passed on to a Master Painter who, along with Lowenthal, chooses the vibrant and unique colors for the figurine. The figurines are then produced in a specific edition size, a process that may undergo change in the near future (see *Secondary Market Overview*).

Before the figurines are complete, they are marked with the appropriate logo on the bottom, as well as with a fitting or whimsical quote. The edition number and piece number are handwritten ("12E/325"), while the style number, title, copyright year

Collectors' Corner

and "The Boyds Collection Ltd." are printed just beneath. The Dollstone pieces have a notation identifying the pieces as part of a special "series" (Victorian Series, Home Again Series, etc.). While The Boyds Collection Ltd. acknowledges these "series" as informal groupings, they are not considered official collections.

All pieces feature their own special mark that identifies them as authentic Boyds collectibles: a paw print (Bearstones and Shoe Box Bears), a star (Folkstones), shoe prints (Dollstones) and a tree for the Folkstone pieces in the *Santa & Friends* grouping. Originally, the edition numbers of The Shoe Box Bears were printed inside the joint of one of the legs. Because of the difficulty of this process, the 1996 pieces were the only ones with the edition number printed right on the bear. Pieces produced after January 1, 1997, will have their edition number printed on the certificate enclosed in the box.

| Bearstone mark | Folkstone mark | Dollstone mark | Santa & Friends mark |

All resin pieces are protected by foam packing and come with a small card describing the production process. The Bearstone pieces come in green boxes with maroon trim; Folkstones have tall, maroon boxes with green trim; and the Dollstones come in very elegant Victorian-style tan boxes with a washed look. The Shoe Box Bears are packaged in small "shoeboxes" that are covered in brown wrapping paper. The boxes feature drawings of the bears and The Shoe Box Bears logo. All boxes feature the appropriate collection logo, a statement of authenticity signed by Gary Lowenthal and thoughtful and amusing quotes from writers, political figures and other prominent people. On the bottom of the box are the copyright year, address for The Boyds Collection Ltd. and a sticker featuring a line drawing of the piece, the title and the UPC symbol.

Collectors' Corner

Bearstones range from $13 to $35, except for limited editions, which are generally higher. Ornaments are approximately $10, waterglobes around $36 and the new votives are around $26. Most Folkstones are under $20, with limited editions and larger pieces reaching the $35 range. The Dollstones range from $14 to $30, although the limited edition pieces range from $47 to $55, while the only Dollstone waterglobe costs around $40 and the votive, $25. The Shoe Box Bears range from $10 to $19.

2. Plush Animals

Like their resin cousins, every Boyds plush animal is first conceived in Gary Lowenthal's mind and then sketched into life. Once the drawing is evaluated and refined, often numerous times, it is sent to a seamstress. Next, depending on the detail involved in its creation, the seamstress cuts the pattern for the animal either by hand or with a machine, and each is then sewn and individually stuffed. Features such as noses, mouths and paws are also individually hand-stitched so that each and every animal brings its own unique qualities to the collection.

Most plush characters come with a tag that identifies the series and a space where retailers can write the name of the animal. On the back side of the tag, there is often an anecdote about the origin of the teddy bear or the story of how Boyds creates their own. The packaging of Boyds plush keeps with the simplicity of the animals themselves; they are not put into fancy boxes but are instead packed in bags. Prices for the Boyds plush vary depending on the size and style of bear. The smaller bears start around $6, while the 16" and 21" bears can reach up to about $50. Most plush characters, however, are in the $15 to $25 range.

COLLECTOR'S
VALUE GUIDE™

Collectors' Corner

Introducing . . . The Collectors' Club!

In June of 1996, The Boyds Collection Ltd. announced its very own collectors' club in response to the rapidly growing popularity of the line.

The Loyal Order of Friends of Boyds™

The Boyds Collection Ltd.
P.O. Box 4386, F.o.B. Dept.
Gettysburg, PA 17325-4386

The charter year of the club runs until December 31, 1997. Collectors who join in the charter year will earn the honored title "Original F.o.B.," while those who join after December 31, 1997 will be known as "Genuine F.o.B's." With a $30 membership fee, the collector is entitled to one year of membership which offers several benefits, including two exclusive pieces: a Bearstone figurine, "Uncle Elliot . . . The Head Bean Wants You," which is gift boxed and comes with a Certificate of Authenticity; and "Raeburn," a 6" jointed plush bear. Members will also have the opportunity to purchase two exclusive pieces which will be available in April, 1997: a Bearstone figurine, "Velma Q. Berriweather . . . The Cookie Queen" and the plush "Velma Q. Berriweather," an 11" fully-jointed bear. A pawprint and "F.o.B." will be embroidered on Velma's paw, making her extra special (see page 72 for listings in the *Value Guide* section).

Collectors also receive a Bearstone pin, a membership card, an official F.o.B. tattoo, a national directory of Boyds Bears dealers, a color catalog order form, a Boyds Bears and Friends Product List and a one-year subscription to *The Boyds Bears Retail Inquirer*, a newsletter which features information on new releases, retirements and tidbits of Boyds history – all written in that unique "Head Bean" way! To join the club, use the application at the back of this book or check with your local retailer.

In addition to the officially sponsored club there are also independent local chapter in which collectors have the chance to meet other Boyds enthusiasts in their own neighborhood. Club members commonly buy, sell and trade pieces, organize trips to collector events and even publish their own newsletters. Ask your favorite retailer if there is a Boyds Bears club in your area – or start your own!

COLLECTOR'S
VALUE GUIDE™

1E—a notation on the bottom of Boyds resin figurines distinguishing the "first edition" pieces. These are generally the most sought-after pieces in the Boyds collection (see definition for *edition*).

2E, 3E, etc.—notations identifying figurines subsequent to "1E" pieces (see definition for *edition*).

Bronze Paw Dealers—the first of three tiers of Boyds retailers who receive priority shipping and larger allotments of certain pieces.

bottomstamp—identifying marks on the underside of Boyds resin pieces. This includes collection logos, copyright years, quotes or phrases, etc.

catalog exclusives—The Boyds Collection Ltd. has offered early releases of several "next year's introductions" to a group of retailers who participate in a selected gift catalog.

collectibles—anything and everything that is "able to be collected," whether it's figurines, dolls...or even *beer bottle caps* can be considered a "collectible," but it is generally recognized that a true collectible should be something that increases in value over time.

edition—the numbering system used by The Boyds Collection Ltd. to keep track of the number of resin pieces they produce. There are 3,600 pieces in every Bearstone and Folkstone edition, and 4,800 pieces in every Dollstone edition. The edition numbers are handwritten on the bottoms of the figurines.

exchange—a secondary market service which lists pieces that collectors wish to buy or sell. The exchange works as a middleman and usually requires a commission.

Gift Creations Concepts (GCC)— a syndicated catalog group which includes over 300 retail stores nationwide. Exclusive pieces and early releases are commonly available through these retailers.

Gold Paw Dealers—the highest tier of Boyds retailers who receive priority shipping and larger allotments of certain pieces.

GRS—a notation that identifies pieces that have been made from a mold that has been "resculpted." This mark is also seen as "RS."

International Collectible Exposition—national collectible shows held in Rosemont, Illinois each June or July, and in April alternating between Long Beach, California one year (next up in 1997) and Secaucus, New Jersey the next (1998).

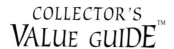

issue price—the retail price of an item when it is first introduced.

jointed—a piece whose arms, legs or head move. Many of the plush animals are jointed as are the resin Shoe Box Bears.

limited edition (LE)—a piece scheduled for a determined production quantity or time period (ex. the Dollstone figurine "The Amazing Bailey . . . 'Magic Show At 4'" is limited to 1997 production).

mint condition—piece offered on the secondary market that is in like-new condition. Mint-in-box means the piece comes in its original box.

N.A.L.E.D.—National Association of Limited Edition Dealers, a retail trade association.

open edition—a piece with no predetermined limitation on time or size of production run.

primary market—the conventional collectibles purchasing process in which collectors buy directly from dealers at issue price.

Premier Edition—the edition marking given to Dollstone pieces originally introduced and sold on QVC.

retired—a piece which is taken out of production, never to be made again, usually followed by a scarcity of the piece and a rise in value on the secondary market (see definition for *secondary market*).

RS—a notation that identifies pieces that have been made from a mold that has been "resculpted." This mark is also seen as "GRS."

secondary market—the source for buying and selling collectibles according to basic supply-and-demand principles ("pay what the market will bear"). Popular pieces which have retired or pieces with low edition numbers can appreciate in value far above the original retail issue price. Pieces are sold through local and national newspaper ads, collector newsletters and through swap & sells at collector meetings.

sudden death retirement—the sudden, "unplanned" removal of a piece from production. Retirement is effective at the time the announcement is made instead of at the end of the year as with normal retirements.

Silver Paw Dealers—the second of three tiers of Boyds retailers who receive priority shipping and larger allotments of certain pieces.

swap & sell—event where collectors meet to buy, sell or trade items.

variations—pieces that have color or design changes from the "original" piece. Some of these changes are minor, while some are important enough to affect the value of a piece on the secondary market.

COLLECTOR'S
VALUE GUIDE™